INNER (*HEART*) HEALING
AND

Freedom

M Y R A C. C A R D E N

COPYRIGHT PAGE

Printed in the United States of America

First Printing, 2024

ISBN 979-8-9913326-0-6

Myra Carden
Whiting, Indiana
soteriaministries01@gmail.com

www.soteriaministries.net

Designed by: DeLisa New Williams

Image by: Freepik <https://www.freepik.com/free-ai-image/broken-heart-studio_94937100.htm#fromView=search&page=1&position=31&uuid=39669afc-46ea-4712-952c-1558533325c8">

INNER (*HEART*) HEALING
AND
Freedom

M Y R A   C.   C A R D E N

ADVANCE PRAISE

"I first met Myra on the day I got baptized, shortly after I joined the church. It was during a large transition period in my life. I recently left a job, stopped drinking alcohol, and was yearning for something new.

After I gave my testimony and was still wet from the baptism, Myra said that I should enroll in her Inner Healing class. I currently had another class at that time, but I prayed and made the decision to go. During the class, I realized that I held on to a lot of past hurt and regret and felt like moving forward was impossible.

I signed up for one of the personal healing sessions during a very tumultuous time. Myra helped me realize that I've been stuck because of multiple incidents that happened to me when I was younger at the same time. I battled lust, pornography, people pleasing, and not finishing what I started. Now, I am more aware of God's ultimate power and my personal human limitations.

Her (book) will help people see their shortcomings, give them to God, and He will show us how to use them for our growth and to help others do the same."

Daveed Holmes, Owner of Apertrue Photography

INTRO

This ministry was born out of my own personal journey to inner healing. I had been through something traumatic and felt I had nowhere to turn. I tried to find comfort in the church but was met with rejection. I tried to join worship teams at a few different churches, but I was told I was "too old" and that I didn't fit the image they wanted to project because they were trying to set an example of what people wanted to see when they entered the sanctuary, and that since I couldn't dance around in heels, I was rejected. Of course, I couldn't dance around in some heels, so I inquired about playing the keyboard instead. And yet again, I was rejected. There seemed to be more and more rejection, and all the rejection was from the church.

But I refused to give up. I knew God had a plan for me, and He did. I was introduced to a church in Hammond, Indiana where I began attending and eventually joined. But not long after, more rejection. It didn't take long, but I found myself in a really dark place, when I heard the Lord say, "Here you go around that mountain AGAIN." Wait! Did He actually just say that to me? I was astonished, and then suddenly, I recalled many situations that occurred in my life, stretching back to my childhood. These experiences had left me feeling timid, severely rejected, and, worst of all, embarrassed.

Upon reflection, I realized that I shared many similarities with my mother. We both tended to withdraw and give up when hurt or rejected. For instance, my mother had been a choir director and pianist at her church for many years, but she was eventually replaced by someone younger and more experienced. The same situation happened to her again at another church she started attending. The rejection deeply wounded her, and she eventually stopped attending church altogether. I have had similar experiences in my own life, and I know how painful it can be not to feel good enough. Holy Spirit even awakened me one night from a sound sleep to reveal that my grandmother, a Godly Pentecostal-Holiness woman, had also wrestled with the same spirits, such as hurt, rejection, abandonment, and others. Suddenly, everything started to make sense! Holy Spirit showed me how people in the Body of Christ were suffering and failing to reach their full potential because of painful memories from their past. I could now see what was happening.

Church hurt was a tormenting generational cycle in my bloodline and the bondage I was in for six years of living a sinful, carefree lifestyle following my divorce from my ex-husband of 34 years, who was also, you guessed it, a preacher! In 2011, after turning my life back over to God, I realized that my passion was to help people in abusive situations. At a former church, I led several life groups and noticed that I could relate to people who felt trapped in bondage and couldn't find a way to break free. Also, I noticed that it wasn't just victims of abuse who were deeply hurt. Women started coming to my classes who had dealt with rape, abortion, incest, PTSD, family curses, and many other painful experiences. God was showing me how His people were hurting through these traumatic events and were still dealing with the pain, and their hurts began speaking very distinctly to my heart of the hurt in His church.

On the surface, they appeared to have it all together, but inside, they carried heavy burdens from their past that they didn't know how to confront. They would have progressed in their walk with God and then hit another "wall," causing them to regress. I had one beautiful mother who had an abortion after learning that their child either would not have lived or would have been severely handicapped. I had another mother who had been raped over and over as a young girl by her father and had even kept a piece of material from his pajamas; another dear woman of God had also been raped repeatedly by family members while growing up and found it very difficult to have a sexual relationship with her husband. After our life group meetings, I would go home and cry for these dear women who had become like sisters to me due to their enduring pain. My knowledge could only take them so far because life experience was all I knew then. During this period, I began to feel a stirring in my spirit about my purpose and passion. I kept hearing the phrase, "Your passion becomes your purpose."

As the classes grew and we continued to meet, I read from the book "Healing for Damaged Emotions" by Dr. David Seamands, a writer, scholar, and United Methodist Theologian. Dr. Seamands asserted that "people tend to carry deep wounds from the past, primarily situated in their emotions," and he argued that "these wounds continue to shape their lives until they are honestly confronted, addressed, and surrendered to Jesus" (Seamands, David, 1981, Healing for Damaged Emotions, Cook Publishing). After reading this book and receiving revelation, I began to pay closer attention to the requests for prayer, the recurring battles, and the repetitive struggles that people around me were facing. Many of the ladies were experiencing the same situations repeatedly, getting the same results, and engaging in conversations centered on these issues. One such mother repeatedly asked for prayer from the residual effects of her abortion- the guilt; another was dealing with an abusive husband and did not know if leaving him was the right thing to do as a Christian. We seemed to deal with the same issues week after week. I could only take them so far because I knew nothing more.

I embarked on a journey to study inner healing while facilitating another life group. I began reading everything I could get my hands on about "inner healing," from books and studying online to printing material off my computer to learn more about this practice. I even started journaling my story and learned more about inner healing for myself. From my research, I learned that many people struggle with issues from their past, such as trust issues, unforgiveness, anger, church wounds, and generational curses. These people are often stuck in vicious cycles, continuously going around the same mountain. At that time, I focused on women because, from my experience, they were more transparent and willing to open up about their deep inner turmoil than men. However, I've seen men become more ready to begin their inner healing journey through the years.

Now it was time to dive in and help these women find the freedom and healing they longed for. They all received inner healing through faith, prayer, journaling, and endurance. I witnessed these ladies' hearts mend from divorce, turn from desiring to murder their spouse, heal from heavy unforgiveness, overcome childhood sexual abuse, and overcome years of battling rejection from childhood to adulthood. Those were powerful moments, and the best part is that God allows me to keep witnessing His people being healed whenever I hear their testimonies.

My personal inner healing began when I took an online training class through Prophetic Heart Healing with Elise Tarango and had an unexpected and intimate encounter with Jesus as I listened to Elise teach us and lead us into the Presence of Jesus. After that encounter, there was no doubt in my mind that Jesus wants to heal his children's hearts from all of the pain and abuse. I also connected with ConnectUp Ministry - another beautiful inner healing training with Katie Luse. That training changed my life forever. I also had training from Face to Face Ministries who taught the Immaneul Approach for inner healing sessions. From there I felt impressed to go back to school and take classes through *Global Awakening School of Supernatural Ministry*. My study was on their Healing Module and included Physical Healing, Inner Healing and Deliverance. I graduated with a Christian Healing Certified Practitioner diploma. My own inner healing continued while in Global Awakening as we "deep dived" into our own healing as I had to confront my own personal issues and bring them to Jesus. This included being transparent and writing about it, but it didn't stop there- we had to post our issues in class where everyone could read and comment on them, including our Instructor. As I read and gleaned from comments from the other students, and took them to heart, more healing was happening. I learned to get alone and listen to the voice of the Father and have a two-way journaling experience with Him. Oh, the healing that came from doing that was beautiful.

My prayer is the same for you, too! Whatever the reason that brought you to this moment, may your journey to inner healing and freedom begin TODAY.

Before you begin Chapter 1, read "The Wall" by Gloria Jay Evans. "The Wall" is a metaphor/parable used to identify wounds, lies, and defense mechanisms and show how they impede spiritual growth and recovery. When I desperately needed God's healing, this story opened my eyes and heart revealing God's truth about myself. After reading "The Wall", I was inspired to create my own "wall" and be free from all the hurt the Holy Spirit showed me was at the core of my soul.

Since then, many others have constructed their walls and returned ready to begin their work toward their inner healing journey.

Crafting your wall is not a requirement for inner healing; however, the exercise encourages you to allow God to reveal to you the defenses in your own life and with God's help, surrender those defenses in exchange for what God has for you…"inner healing and freedom" from your past.

Take this time to read "The Wall" and ask the Holy Spirit to help you see what's on your own wall.

THE WALL

By: Gloria Jay Evans

I do not know when I first began to build the wall. I suppose it was when it occurred to me that I could keep people out of my life by building a simple wall. The wall would be a kind of boundary, a kind of protection. At first the little wall was only knee high. It was really quite attractive; made of native stone I had found in my life.

The wall was so small that some people did not notice it --- and fell flat on their faces. Others saw it but would step over it and come close to me. I found this uncomfortable. So, I built the wall higher. This was really much better. But soon I found that people would come and rest their arms on the wall while talking to me. Some stayed too long, and some were not my kind of people. And even when I edged the top of the wall with sharp stones, they did not seem to notice.

One day one of them vaulted over the wall and stood right inside. This made me angry. I decided to build the wall higher.

As I continued to build, I became more and more self-sufficient. I painted designs on the stones. I made arcs and colored windows that distorted the light so that one could neither see in nor out.

The Wall pleased me so that I longed to show it to someone --- or explain how I had achieved each design. But I realized that no one had stopped by to talk for some time. Some walked by not seeming to notice me or my wall. Others stood sadly by and watched me build. I thought they were jealous of my Wall, and I resented them, all of them.

One day a man stopped to listen as I explained how I was building the wall. He wanted to come inside to see what I was doing. I explained to him that the whole purpose of the wall was to keep people on the other side. But I could tell he did not understand or care. As he left, I went back to build the wall higher.

I became so absorbed in my wall that I found little time for anything else. I searched my life for new and different stones. I found stones that I didn't even know I had.

The design was particularly important to me. I would build and rebuild until it was just the way I wanted it. Some stones were so dear to me that I polished them carefully several times a day. Then one day I realized the wall was so high that I no longer saw anyone go by. I no longer heard anyone. Everything was quiet.

"Is anyone there?" I yelled.

There was no answer. It was dark inside the wall and the air was foul. I sat there for a long time. It was quiet and dark and lonely. Only the whispers of my memories could be heard.

I thought of those who did not like my wall, who had laughed at it, scorned it, and been jealous of it. I sat in the shadows and listened for someone to come and tell me that they really liked it. But it was dark and quiet. *Incredibly quiet.*

I do not know how long I sat in the shadow of my memories, but one day I noticed that one of the stones did not match as well as I had thought, and the wall was crooked. This was too much. I had thought my wall was perfect. But it was not. Frantically I examined the wall and, sure enough, there were other imperfections.

To add to the pain of my discovery, one day someone yelled from the other side. "Your wall is ugly. It is twisted and gray and misshapen!" It was the day the flower fell at my feet that I began to cry. I ran to the wall and climbed to see who had thrown it over. By the time I reached the top, no one was there. I returned to the flower and sat for a long time looking at its perfection. I began to see the folly of my wall and its imperfection.

Floods of tears brought me to my knees. "Oh, I am so alone, my wall is too high. My wall is imperfect and ugly. Everything is in vain. I have nothing left. Won't someone help me --- Please?"

Then a strange thing happened. Something inside me stirred as a baby quickens in its mother's womb. And in the stillness of my broken world, I knew in my whole being a blessed presence. I knelt there in wonder that God would come to me. And I wept with joy that I was not alone --- and that my darkness had been penetrated by his blessed light.

For days I stood in the joy of his presence. My wall shone with the warmth of his light, and I no longer felt cold and alone. I knew that he had watched me build my wall and that He had waited patiently for me to see it was in vain.

Finally, it occurred to me that He would know why my wall was so ugly. When I asked Him, He began to teach me? Day by day He showed me my error. He gave the stones names. "This stone is jealousy. You must remove it." Sometimes I would be reluctant. For days I would protest. This was my favorite stone. It was one I had saved and cherished for years. When I was finally ready, He helped me remove the stone.

One day when we had removed one of the heavier stones, a hand came through the opening. "Take it," He said.

Hesitantly I took the hand. For a long time, I stood in the warmth of that grasp. Somehow, I knew the hand and the one behind it had been waiting for an opening in my wall. There stirred in me a hunger and a longing for human comfort. At first, I thought His presence within my wall was enough. But with the coming of the hand clasp, I knew He had come to tear the wall down. A part of me wanted to spring forth but another part of me cried out in fear. Why couldn't I keep a part of the wall? His presence was enough. I looked at all the stones I had collected throughout my life. Some were still on the wall. The others, He stacked neatly in a corner. If I ever chose to rebuild the wall, I could. I begged Him to throw them away, but he told me that in them, I could test my strength. How they tempted me!

One day when He did not seem to be around, I dashed over and picked up a cherished stone to rebuild my wall. It was then I realized that if I were to be strong enough to live without the wall, I would have to know the stones were there. I would have to know the name of each one. In knowing their names, I could not use them again without betraying Him.

As we removed more stones, the light came in. And His light would shine out. I began to look through the open places. I could see things I had not noticed for a long time --- dewdrops, ladybugs, sunbeams, and blades of grass. He told me many things and gave me gifts. The more I talked to Him the more I wanted to talk to Him. I saw things I had never seen before and heard things I had never heard before.

One day as I was standing by an open place, a man stopped to talk. I told him about the blessed presence and how He had changed my life. The man said he understood. "But," he said, "If that is true, why do you have this block of resentment in your wall? I cannot see Him. The stone blocks the way."

I looked and sure enough, one of my most prized rocks lay directly in front of me covering nearly one side of the wall. It had been one of the first stones I had placed. It was a large conglomerate of disillusionment, childishness, stubbornness, and other petty stones. I asked the man if he would help me remove it. I was so ashamed (that) the blessed presence might see this large rock. The man did loosen the stone and I thanked him as he went on his way. I wondered how I could ever remove that stone without help.

I really tried. I tugged and tugged and struggled and struggled but it only moved slightly. I sat down in despair. I knew the man was right. The stone must be removed.

"Oh dear," I said. "How can I ever remove this one? It is so big, and I am so weak."

"You cannot move it," He said.

"But I must," I replied. "The man said he could hardly believe you were here with that stone in the wall."

"If you really want the stone removed, I will remove it." We went carefully over to the wall and chipped away each small stone until the large one was diminished.

Even with the stone of resentment gone, people kept stumbling over debris and remnants of the wall as they walked through my life. There was a woman who knew Him and had let Him tear down her wall. She walked in and sat down on one of the stones. I told her what He had done for me, and she told me what He had done for her. I told her how I had suffered so (much) and that I would never forget how forsaken and lonely I had felt inside my wall.

"Yes," she said, "self-pity is a terrible thing."

When she left, I found the stone of self-pity in my wall. It was wet with my tears. I dried it off and laid it with the other stones. The wall was almost demolished. I looked around at all the world I could see. I thought of His great love for me and breathed a deep sigh of satisfaction and pride that I should have come so far.

"Look how much I have accomplished," I thought. "How much better I know Him than some of those others out there. Poor unenlightened ones who do not know Him nearly as well as I. It is so easy. Why can't they see?"

Overwhelmed by all He had done for me and all He had taught me, I stood upon one of the remaining stones and began to tell anyone who passed by what the blessed presence had done for me. I was appalled that no one seemed to hear or understand what I was saying. I told them how dark and lonely it had been inside the wall. And how He had come to help me tear it down. How vain it was to build walls. I noticed others working on walls and ran over to plead with them to stop, but no one would listen. In my frustration I cried out, "Why can't they hear? Why can't they understand? Why can't they believe me?"

I lay face down on the stone I had stood upon. It was extremely large, highly polished. It was my great prize. It was more than life size.

"Do you want the answer to your question?" He asked.

"You know I do," I sighed.

"Raise your head and look at the stone you are lying upon."

I raised my head and gasped for I saw my own reflection in the massive stone. There was pride in my look and manner. I knew the stone was pride. Quietly, we removed it.

Now we could see beyond the meadow and a path led forth from where I stood. Then He said a strange thing. "Now you must go. I will go with you and yet I will stay here."

"But I don't want to leave," I protested. "The wall still stands. There are other stones to remove. I want to be here with you."

"I said I would go with you. There is an opening in the wall for you to come and go. Do you remember the flower that fell at your feet, the hand that you clasped, the woman who showed you self-pity or the man who showed you resentment?" "Oh yes," I sighed, "Oh yes."

"Then you must go and do likewise. For to whom much is given, much is expected. Wherever you go I go with you. And whenever you come back here to be tempted or to remove more stones I will be here."

So, I went forth. Soon I saw a wall builder. He had just started to build his wall. I saw pain and hurt in his face --- and confusion in his frenzy to build. I leaned against the wall wanting to tell him I understood. But the stones were placed so that the sharp edges cut me, and I retreated in pain. I stood by the wall nursing my wounds. In sadness I watched him build. Soon his wall was so high I could not see him, and my heart ached because I knew it was dark and lonely inside. I called to him, but he could not hear. The ugliness of the wall was unbelievable. I reached out and touched it, leaned against it. I don't know how long I was there but one day I heard someone yell, "Your wall is ugly. It is twisted and gray and misshapen."

Strangely, though, I had never heard a sound from the wall before. Great racking sobs exploded from inside. Tears streamed down my face, and I cried out in frustration, "Won't you help him please? Please?"

I thought my heart would break. In desperation I looked about. If only I could give him a gift to ease his pain. I looked down to find a small flower at my feet. Hastily I plucked it and threw it over the wall. Then the sobbing stopped, and I knew a great peace, for in some strange way I knew that the blessed presence had come to him and that my aching heart and the gift of the flower had helped bring it about. I knew that soon there would be an opening in the wall, and I could grasp his hand. I knew, too, that he might never know that it was I who was there. But it really did not matter for in some wonderful way, I had become a part of every man's life. Through the blessed presence we would all become one. Somehow, I knew I would never be the same.

I returned to my wall and the blessed presence was there. Together we removed the stones of fear, mistrust, and indifference. He said, "Now you begin to understand love. Without love, all the things I have told you would be meaningless. You will begin to live in peace and understanding. You will learn gentleness and kindness. But it will take time. I will always be with you."

So it was that I went forth reaching out --- sometimes just waiting beside a wall, sometimes tossing a flower, sometimes grasping a hand.

There are days that I return to my wall. I touch the stacked stones and examine the remnants of my wall. At times I am filled with a desire to rebuild it, but we talk, and He helps me to be strong. Sometimes we remove another stone.

It is strange that I began to recognize others like myself. When I see someone with a flower, I know that it will be thrown over a wall.

Sometimes I see someone standing by a wall sadly watching a wall builder. I see those who are sitting on stones explaining what kind of stones they have used.

I know the blessed presence is with them, too. We pass on the path and a great love passes between us. I see peace in their eyes and faith in their hearts and I know that someday the walls will be down, and we will all walk free from place to place --- The Great Family of God.

THE WALL, A PARABLE is a fully illustrated book by Gloria Jay Evans. Published by EE Books, 1999 and Word Books, 1977. Copyright 1977 Word Books and 1999 Gloria Jay Evans.

May your journey to heart healing and freedom begin TODAY

Who's voice is it anyway?

WHEN DEALING WITH ISSUES, AND NOT KNOWING WHETHER YOU ARE HEARING GOD'S VOICE OR SATAN'S VOICE, HERE IS A REFERENCE TO HELP YOU. YOU CAN REFER BACK TO THIS ANYTIME YOU NEED TO.

God's Voice

- ☐ STILLS YOU
- ☐ LEADS YOU
- ☐ REASSURES YOU
- ☐ ENLIGHTENS YOU
- ☐ ENCOURAGES YOU
- ☐ COMFORTS YOU
- ☐ CALMS YOU
- ☐ CONVICTS YOU

Satan's Voice

- ☐ RUSHES YOU
- ☐ PUSHES YOU
- ☐ FRIGHTENS YOU
- ☐ CONFUSES YOU
- ☐ DISCOURAGES YOU
- ☐ WORRIES YOU
- ☐ OBSESSES YOU
- ☐ CONDEMNS YOU

Hitting the "pause" button at any point in your day and going to the Word, journal, or prayer closet to settle your heart will bring peace and assurance.

———

"INNER HEALING DOES

NOT *erase* A MEMORY

OR *change* YOUR

PERSONAL HISTORY"

———

CHAPTER 1

WHAT IS INNER HEALING?

Inner Healing, as Dr. Charles Kraft, Professor of Prayer Ministry and Spiritual Warfare at Fuller Seminary, puts it, is a "deep-level healing" of the mind, emotions, painful memories, and dreams. Inner Healing is the process through prayer whereby you are set free from resentment, rejection, self-pity, depression, guilt, fear, sorrow, hatred, inferiority, condemnation, worthlessness, and so forth. When healing happens on a deeper level, the spirit is also healed.

It should really be called "prayer and prophetic for sanctification and transformation." Deep-level healing, or Inner Healing, is a ministry of Holy Spirit's power to bring healing and freedom to the whole person, spirit, emotions, and body. It focuses on healing the hurts held in those memories, often by helping you experience Jesus' presence in the memories while handing Him the hurts.

Inner healing is not merely a way to restore hurting people, though it does that. It is a ministry within the Body of Christ that enables Believers to come to more effective and continual death on the Cross and resurrection into the fullness of life in Christ. It is a tool the Lord uses to mature His people. Inner healing is the "application of the crucified and resurrected life of Jesus and His blood to those parts of my heart and yours that did not fully get the "message" when we first received Jesus as our Lord and Savior." It is evangelism to the unbelieving hearts of Believers. Notice I did not say "to unbelieving hearts" but to "unbelieving hearts of *Believers*."

Some areas deep in your heart have not believed and accepted the good news of your death and rebirth in Him. The fullness of His work has not yet happened for you. Yes, you are a new creature in Him, but some of your old self-centered, selfish character continues to act in its ugly old ways as though you had never received Him as Lord. It is a tool of prayer (and the prophetic) to make salvation fully effective in all dimensions of your life and character. In like manner, when you received Jesus as Lord of your life, positionally, you possess the perfection of your soul. But you must yet cross your own inner Jordans, kill your giants, and conquer the fenced and walled areas of your stony heart to possess what you already own. Inner healing is a discipline of prayer to accomplish that task. In Deliverance and Inner Healing by Sanford & Sanford (2008), it is the discipline of *digging deep under the guidance of the Holy Spirit to discover whatever roots might be springing back to life and to bring them to "effective death on the cross."* Inner healing is sanctification!

In Luke 4:18, Jesus declares that *He is uniquely anointed to bring healing to the broken places in people's hearts, to set captives free, and to lead prisoners into liberty.* Successful inner healing is more about the journey and the process of becoming whole. It is not an instant fix to life's ailments because healing takes time. (Eivaz, Jennifer, *Inner Healing and Deliverance Handbook*, pg37). Jesus brings restoration to lives. Inner Healing deals with your response to hurts and memories from the past, including repressed (hidden) memories. Hidden parts of your heart that did **not** believe the Good News when your mind and spirit heard and responded to when you were converted. Those hurts and memories may affect your lives in the form of bad memories, a feeling of worthlessness and inferiority, fears and anxieties, the inability to feel loved and accepted, and so much more! They may come from such things as separation from a parent through illness, divorce, or death (which can be experienced as rejection) or the experiences of failure or lack. It can also come from such things as overwhelming fear, abuse, or a family history of problems such as alcoholism, violence, sexual abuse, church abuse, involvement in the occult, or any unresolved burden of guilt. Many Christians cannot live the Gospel because they have believed **only** with their mind. *Their faith has not yet conquered their heart completely.*

Some of these hurts come from the fact that you are living in a fallen world. Events happen, such as accidents, disease, poverty, and natural disasters that are not of deliberate choice. Hurts can come from your own wrong choices and responses. Memories are often pushed below your conscious thinking, where they stay, and are felt in debilitating ways (repressed). These memories can express themselves in your life as fear, anger, anxiety, resentment, self-hate, guilt, unforgiveness, an inability to trust, persistent, irrational beliefs, and so forth. *When you suppress the hurt so that you can cope, and the memory is not dealt with and remains, it will eventually hinder you. Healing of memories, as taught by some, says you should erase the old. Neither true healing nor transformation ever erases the past.* Inner healing does **not** erase a memory or change your personal history! However, it enables you to cherish even the worst moments in your life, for through them, God has inscribed eternal lessons onto your heart and prepared you to minister to all who have suffered in the same way. (Heb. 2:18) You will know you are healed when you can look back on everything with "gratitude.

The "Inner Healing and Freedom" approach to emotional (heart) healing teaches you the many areas of emotional hurt and how to identify them by giving you symptoms, causes, and scenarios. The work of inner healing is the application of the Blood, the Cross, AND the resurrection life of our Lord Jesus Christ to those stubborn dimensions of believers' hearts that have refused the redemption their minds and spirits requested when they invited Jesus in! I think you should read that sentence again! You do not always do as Jesus says because your mind has not yet been renewed, and you have not yet been "transformed." This transformation is the process of sanctification. Hopefully, some of you will understand that. Let's look at Romans 7:15-20: [15] *I do not understand what I do. For what I want to do I do not do, but what I hate I do. [16] And if I do what I do not want to do, I agree that the law is good. [17] As it is, it is no longer I myself who do it, but it is sin living in me. [18] For I know that good itself does not dwell in me, that is, in my sinful nature. [a]*

For I have the desire to do what is good, but I cannot carry it out. [19] For I do not do the good I want to do, but the evil I do not want to do—this I keep on doing. [20] Now if I do what I do not want to do, it is no longer I who do it, but it is sin living in me that does it. Have you ever found yourself saying those exact things to yourself? Have you found yourself doing things that you don't want to do, and those things you do want to do, you can't or won't do? You will understand that scripture better as we get into the meat of these lessons.

I know you already read this, but let's read it again, and this time, out loud: ***Inner healing does NOT erase a memory or change your personal history!*** However, it does enable you to cherish even the worst moments in your life, for through them, God has inscribed eternal lessons onto your heart and prepared you to minister to all who have suffered in the same way. (Heb 2:18) You will know you are healed when you can look back on everything with "gratitude."

Dr. David Seamands, a Methodist theologian to whom I was first introduced to inner healing, says in his book: *There is something you need to understand, and that is that the Gospel is most practical and gets right down to where you live. (I Cor. 2:2) As Americans, we have been weaned on indiscipline, indecency, and sensuality. We are living in modern Corinth. In our society, it is difficult for anyone to grow to young adulthood without suffering some damage. There are scores of young men and women who were fed a lot of false and harmful ideas/information by well-meaning but ignorant parents, preachers, authority figures. Now, they are unfit for marriage, unable to be husbands or wives who can live without fear, guilt, and shame. Damaged? Yes, badly. God has divine repairs and healing for you.*

We believe in the scripture Romans 8:26 about the Holy Spirit who "helpeth our infirmities." Many modern translations use "weaknesses" or "cripplings" in place of the word infirmities. One meaning of the word "help" has a medical connotation, suggesting the way a nurse helps in the healing process. So, it is not simply "to take hold of on the other side," which is the literal meaning of that verb, but that the Holy Spirit becomes your partner AND helper and works along with us in mutual participation for your healing." (Seamands, David, 1981, *Healing for Damaged Emotions*, Cook Publishing)

These general Biblical principles must be followed throughout this journey for you to receive complete healing for those damaged emotions and repressed memories:

1. Face your problems head-on; **[TRUTH, HONESTY, VULNERABILITY, TRANSPARENCY]**

2. Accept your **responsibility** in the matter

3. Ask YOURSELF: "Do I **WANT** to be healed?"

4. Forgive **everyone** who is involved in your problem

5. Forgive **YOURSELF**

6. Ask the Holy Spirit to show you your problem and how to **pray**

What should I expect to learn about inner healing?

You will learn that Inner healing is simply this: **Evangelizing**, **Sanctifying**, and **Transforming**. We are converting a *character structure* into the nature of our Lord Jesus Christ by changing the body of Christ into a "mature man, to the measure of the stature which belongs to the fullness of Christ" (Ephesians 4:13). Inner Healing allows Jesus to take the wounds and hurts of your past and heal those deep hurtful wounds caused by trauma and abuse that are just too heavy to cope with in life.

Inner Healing is needed when the false identity is rooted in some *emotional wound from the past*. You can ask Jesus to walk back with you to the time you were hurt and to free you from the effects of that wound in this present time. This process will involve two things: **A.)** bringing the things that have hurt you into the light. (Usually, this is best done with another person, and **B.)** praying and asking the Lord to heal the binding effects of those hurtful incidents of the past. There will be a need for forgiveness of the offending party, and there will be a need to receive healing from Jesus regarding the inner hurt, and there may also be a need for deliverance.

Trauma or abuse can be an entry point for demons. When someone says they are tormented by anxiety, fear, guilt, anger, or any other emotion, there is a strong possibility that they have deep soul wounds and are being tormented by demons and need deep-level healing. Isaiah 61 speaks of setting the captives free and binding up the brokenhearted. Inner Healing goes to those broken places, the hurts, the painful emotions, and binds up the broken heart.

Inner Healing is a Tool for Sanctification.

Processing through forgiveness, repentance, and rejecting the lies you have believed is a very sanctifying process. As you strip away all the broken ways of thinking and the faulty foundations, a redeemed mind, healthy life patterns, and firm foundations begin to develop. The main components of Inner Healing Prayer are **Forgiveness, Repentance, Closing Doors**, and replacing lies with the **Truth**. Again, it is the application of the Blood **AND** the Cross **AND** the resurrection life of Jesus to those stubborn dimensions of believers' hearts that have refused the redemption their minds and spirits requested when they invited Jesus in!

Revival preachers have claimed that from the moment you receive Jesus as Lord, your entire character is changed, and you become a new creature. Positionally, that is true. Paul, however, made it clear that you must "work out your salvation (healed and transformed character) as the "outcome of your faith." (I Pet. 1:9), not the beginning. "The prevalence of that truncated (not preaching the three-fold Gospel of regeneration, justification, and sanctification) has meant that leaders being raised up today have largely remained unaware of the necessity of bringing their fleshly practices to death on the cross after being Born Again (Col 3:9-10) that is SAD!

Deliverance and Inner Healing are ONE!

Deliverance casts out evil spirits, also known as "demons ." Jesus spent ⅓ of His ministry casting out demons and setting people free from torment. Evil spirits affect humanity on different levels. While some evil spirits are from without (outside of us), others can be from within (inside of us). Negative spirits can come through by demonization or possession. Possession is when a demon has a hold and complete control over an individual. Demonization is when one has a demon inside of them influencing their actions and lives without actually possessing them (i.e., someone plagued by pornography). They seek help and go to a team that specializes in deliverances. The Deliverance Team/Ministry prays and binds a "perverse spirit" and commands it to leave that person. When the demonic spirit leaves, the man/woman voices immediate peace, release, and relief. They are free. This process is how the majority of deliverance ministry takes place. They were not possessed but instead were *demonized* by a spirit that lived inside of them and influenced them in powerful ways. More often, people are demonized rather than possessed, and when they come for prayer, the person gets better rapidly through deliverance.

Cindy Jacobs, a renowned prophetic intercessor and co-founder of General of Intercession, deals with supernatural life and teaches on the demonic realm. Here, she lists several causes of demonization:

1. Bitterness and unforgiveness
2. Iniquity (including sins of the fathers and past generations)
3. The occult
4. Sin (particularly sexual sin as it is a union that transfers spirits)
5. Trauma
6. Abuse

According to Cindy, here is a more in-depth look at how you can open yourself up to being demonized and/or possessed. She breaks it down further into categories:

- Regression: a person no longer has a desire for the things of God
- Repression: absence of joy in the individual's life
- Suppression: a general sense of melancholy or lethargy
- Depression: state of worthlessness and hopelessness involving loss of appetite and loss of sleep
- Oppression: the sense of being weighed down by an unseen force
- Obsession: persistent disturbing preoccupation with an often unreasonable idea or feeling; this changes the mind and calls what is evil GOOD
- Demonization: the individual has given demons the right to dwell inside of them by the sins of their flesh.

Noted German theologian, the late Kurt Koch, who was also a minister, evangelist, and counselor to those suffering from the occult in its various forms, identified eight signs of demonic possession:

1. Demons are living inside the individual and seem to have control
2. Unusual or supernatural strength
3. Visible conflict within the possessed person
4. Opposition to the things of God

5. Clairvoyance: they can identify Jesus even though they have never met him before; they know hidden or secret things

6. Ability to speak in voices not their own and languages they do not know

7. Immediate, instantaneous

8. Transference: the legion that was cast into pigs and destroyed the herd was a sign of possession.

Deliverance of these individuals is possible but often takes longer and is much more involved. A novice in the deliverance ministry should only attempt this with the help of a trained professional minister. Never put a recipient on display- even with Inner Healing prayer. It is to be done in private!

Since many problems we've experienced in our lives go back to the womb (in utero), sin is not the issue. The issue is the "brokenness" behind it. When we get to the root, the sin gets taken care of.

The Goals of Inner Healing

Get to the Root

Many things that keep people in bondage are hidden deep beneath the surface. (That's the way the devil likes it!) People struggle mightily with unforgiveness, anxiety, fear, anger, and other negative emotions, but yet are at a complete loss as to why they are there in the first place. Heb. 12:15 tells us to "see to it that no one comes short of the grace of God; that no root of bitterness springing up causes trouble, and by it many be defiled." It was His finished work on the Cross. Your sin was washed away, and your flesh was dealt a death blow. Your flesh refuses to stay dead, so we will dig deep, under the guidance of the Holy Spirit, and discover whatever roots might spring back to life and bring them to effective death. We pull up roots, replace lies with truth, and close the doors that need to be closed.

Isaiah 61:1 says, "*The Spirit of the Lord God is upon me because He has anointed and commissioned me to bring good news to the humble and afflicted; He has sent me to bind up the wounds of the brokenhearted, and the proclaim release from confinement and condemnation to the physical and spiritual captives. (Amp)*

Isaiah prophesied that one of the ministries of Jesus would be to "heal the brokenhearted." Please understand that the word "broken" used in that verse literally means "shattered into separate pieces." When you can grasp that scripture, that you can be healed on the inside, your heart, and your emotions, you can expect your physical healing to be manifested. The body cannot be fully healed while it is still reflecting the inner pain of an unhealed trauma. Your spirit and soul (your inner being) have been shattered, but you will walk in healing! Physical and emotional.

<u>REPEAT THIS AGAIN:</u> *Inner Healing does **NOT** erase a memory or change your personal history! But it does enable you to cherish even the worst moments in your life, for through them, God has inscribed eternal lessons onto your heart and prepared you to minister to all who have suffered in the same way. (Heb 2:18) You will know you are healed when you can look back on everything with "gratitude."*

Realign with the Truth

God has built spiritual and physical laws into His creation. They apply to everyone's lives whether they know them or not. Love is the essential ingredient that fulfills all of these laws. By realigning people with the tools of love, forgiveness, mercy, and grace and applying them to the root issues, those roots begin to lose their power and die. The damaging effect they have had on lives subsides. That which was out of rhythm with God's perfect design is removed.

Walk in Victory

The Cross was the final victory over sin and death. Victory was and is always there for the taking, yet sin and death are still hard at work to keep you from truly experiencing the freedom Christ has brought you. By healing the areas of your heart that have not yet agreed with this truth, you will experience the true freedom that God intended.

You can now experience victory and lift the illusion of defeat...

"*You* ARE WHAT GOD SAYS ABOUT *you,* BUT THE MIND REMEMBERS WHAT "USED" TO BE TRUE ABOUT *you.*"

CHAPTER 2

THE MIND: WHERE THE BATTLE IS REALLY FOUGHT

It is shocking how many Believers are pulled down simply because of the thoughts they allow to control their minds. Many Believers can access a great deal of spiritual victory simply by changing how they think and controlling the thoughts that flow through their minds. As you continue reading, you will understand more about your mind and its importance to your inner healing journey.

Your mind controls your emotions.

Many people do not believe or understand how their mind controls their emotions. And if you're one of those unbelievers, try going through something traumatic and not have your MIND give you 100 different scenarios in addition to creating scenes and playing them out in your MIND. It's impossible. According to memory specialists, the mind stores our experiences and memories in pictures rather than words. It's best for your inner healing journey to deal with those hurtful memories in pictures because of the 'amygdala'; they can't be healed with just words alone.

The amygdala is a little gray mass in the brain's temporal lobe that functions in emotional and autonomic responses associated with fear. It also processes and consolidates memories. *"The amygdala is commonly thought to form the core of a neural system for **processing fearful and threatening stimuli**, including **detection of threat and activation of appropriate fear-related behaviors** in response to threatening or dangerous stimuli." https://www.pnas.org/*

Whatever you pay attention to will become magnified in your eyes and life. Whatever you give heed to will become more important to you. After all, as Nehemiah 8:10 tells us, *"For the joy of the LORD is your strength.* That is why the enemy tries to get your mind and thoughts derailed and off of the truth that is in God's Word. He tries to get you to worry about things that, in reality, you have no reason to be worried about! Rom. 12:1-2 says, *"I beseech you therefore brethren, by the mercies of God, that you present your bodies a living sacrifice, holy, acceptable to God, which is your reasonable service. And do NOT be conformed to this world but be ye transformed by the renewing of your mind, that you may prove what is that good and acceptable and perfect will of God."* What your human spirit comes to know as true, your mind has to be "retrained" to accept and believe.

You are what God says about you, but the mind remembers what "used" to be true about you. Unless your mind is renewed (choosing to believe what God's **Word** says and not your own preconceived ideas or thoughts) , it will always believe the LIE and fight you over who you are and what you have in Christ. YOU MUST RENEW YOUR MIND!!!! *The demonic realm CANNOT read your mind*, but when those spirits are at work, they will speak to you and try to get you to "verbalize" an opening through your words. You must watch *your words*. There is a kinetic power going to work that's dynamic and energizing in your word *and* the Word. It is released into the realm of the senses as active energy when it comes out of your mouth. According to Ps. 103:20, angels heed the commandment of God when they hear the voice of the Lord:

Bless the Lord, O you his angels, you mighty ones who do His Word, obeying the voice of His Word!

Since the Holy Spirit works in you, angels obey your words when you speak the Word just as they obeyed Jesus' Word when He walked the earth. Quote the Word and add a hardener to the patch that the Holy Spirit healed in your soul! What's a hardener? Like in the natural, when you paint, you add a hardener to form a stronger bond between the surface and the paint. Without the hardener, the paint would take forever to dry, the set-up wouldn't be as cohesive, and it would lack shine. The same applies in the spiritual when we actually speak His Word. That is the hardener we need to add with the Holy Spirit to form the strong bond that heals your soul. When we do this, we choose to believe scripture instead of our circumstances. The promises of God are YES and AMEN. He sent the Holy Spirit to help you heal the dysfunctions of your past by removing the lie of emotional imbalance. The lie is removed when the Holy Spirit shows you what happened in the spirit realm when trauma occurred.

God overwrites trauma with Truth. The Truth comes from the Spirit of Truth, and the Word of Truth is the Holy Spirit that guides Believers into all truths. The Bible says in John 16:13, "But when He, the Spirit of truth, comes, He will guide you into all the truth. He will not speak on his own; He will speak only what He hears, and He will tell you what is yet to come." Once the truth has been sown in your mind through you outwardly speaking the Word with verses related to the remedy, that patch thoroughly heals.

Here's a testimony of what happens when you speak the Word and only the Word over your life to receive inner healing. "A dear sister who came to Inner Healing and Freedom, and boy, she was a mess when she arrived. She was consumed with hurt, bitterness, and unforgiveness. When she arrived, she didn't see how she could get healed from *ALL* that happened to her. She had a beautiful connection with Holy Spirit, and He went deep into her heart and healed things as far back as when she was a young girl. When the session was over, we gave her our "Sealing your Healing" pamphlet, which we pass out after each session. We strongly encouraged her that a breakthrough would come when she spoke God's Word over every situation and replaced all negative thoughts with the Word. She struggled initially but refused to be defeated each day and found scriptures to stand on for everything she was going through. Today, she is one on-fire woman of God. She refused to accept defeat in her life- and decreed the Word of God over every situation she was going through. She says it was no picnic- she fought long and hard for her "heart healing," and God's Word did not let her down. He has healed family relationships, and she now walks in forgiveness with them. Seeing that she is one happy woman is a blessing and joy.

God doesn't want you living dysfunctional lives because of old, ugly memories. Truth overwrites trauma when the Holy Spirit causes you to realize the truth through the "real eyes," the eyes of the Spirit. Once you have seen the Truth, you must build your mental and emotional strength by quoting, meditating, and repeatedly speaking the Word of God aloud. Truth overwrites trauma, heals broken hearts, balances emotions, and heals dysfunctions. The truth comes from the Spirit of Truth and the Word of Truth. It is a two-part remedy: Jesus the Good Samaritan pours in the oil of the Holy Spirit AND the wine of the Word of God. Jesus came to heal the brokenhearted and to set at liberty those who have been traumatized!!! Luke 4:18 (*Wagner, Doris How to Minister Freedom to Others, Dale M. Sides, pg. 144*)

Is it a sin problem? That was dealt with in 1 John 1:9, *"If we confess our sins, He is faithful and just to forgive us our sins, and to cleanse us from all unrighteousness."* In plain English, it does not matter what you have done; if you are willing to take it before the Lord, you can be forgiven! An old song says, "Take your burden to the Lord and leave it THERE." You should try it! You have already been delivered. He paid that price to give you complete victory as you abide in HIM.

Is it a financial problem? Is God your provider? Can He supply all your needs according to HIS riches? Are His riches less than yours? Is it not God that gives the power to gain wealth? Deuteronomy 8:18, "But thou shalt remember the LORD thy God: for it is He that giveth thee power to get wealth, that He may establish his covenant which He swore unto thy fathers, as it is this day."

Do you need healing? Was that not paid for on the cross? Were His stripes not given as ransom for your healing (Isaiah 53:5)? Did not Jesus demonstrate this by healing EVERYBODY who came to Him? (Matthew 8:16-17) Remember Isa 61:1. Physical healing can occur when your shattered heart is healed through prayerfully applying this scripture. Activist and politician Nelson Mandela once said, "Hating someone(unforgiveness) is drinking poison and expecting the other person to die from it." And there is research that has shown that unforgiveness is linked to high blood pressure, weakened immune systems, reduced sleep, chronic pain, arthritis, and cardiovascular problems. So I ask you- why wouldn't you want to be healed?

You cannot believe what you do not know. Did you read that? Did you understand it? You cannot believe what you do not know, so you must first renew your mind to the truth of God's Word. Study the Word and find what it says about you, your life, your healing, your future, and the plans He has for you, your hope, and your future!! Joe McIntyre says in his book, "Who We Are In Christ," *"The first thing you need is knowledge of the Truth.* **WASH** *yourself in it. Let it* **ROLL** *over you and* **UPROOT** *the lie about who you are. Let Father's image of you become YOURS. Take His Word and thank Him that it's true"* (pg. 76)

Perhaps one of the biggest differences between a victorious believer and a depressed or defeated believer is the thoughts that go through your mind daily. Yes, demonic spirits can and do play a crucial role in depression, fear, etc., but many times, all they have to do is get your thoughts derailed, and because of your ignorance of the truth, you begin to become fearful and depressed. The Bible shows us through Saul that evil spirits can fill us with fear and depression when we do not stand on God's Word in faith.

1 Samuel 16:14, "Now the Spirit of the LORD had left Saul, and the LORD sent a tormenting spirit that filled him with depression and fear." (NLT)

Does God want you to be depressed? No! He wants you to be full of joy! (John 15:11)

Does God want you to be fearful? No! He wants you to rest in His love, which expels all fear! (1 John 4:18) You have not been given a spirit of fear again to bondage, but of power, love, and a sound mind! (2 Timothy 1:7)

Does God want you to worry about things? No! His Word tells you not to worry about anything! (Philippians 4:6)

The vital link between thoughts and feelings

I believe Philippians 4:6-8 paints the picture quite well, "Be careful for nothing (Don't worry about anything); but in everything by prayer and supplication with thanksgiving let your requests be made known unto God. And the peace of God, which passeth all understanding, shall keep your hearts and minds through Christ Jesus *(refusing* to worry about anything opens the door to God's peace in our lives). *Finally, brethren, whatsoever things are true, whatsoever things are honest, whatsoever things are just, whatsoever things are pure, whatsoever things are lovely, whatsoever things are of good report; if there be any virtue, and if there be any praise, think on these things* (set your minds on good and positive things that uplift and build you up)." Yes, it can be difficult to "think on these things" when you are in the heat of battle. But I promise you- His Word is true, and if you choose to believe His Word rather than your emotions and the fear that has consumed you, you will be set free and healed. God is not a liar. It is not his nature to lie- He CAN'T lie...... so feel safe knowing that.

Isaiah 26:3 also makes a vital connection between what we fix our minds on and how we feel, *"Thou wilt keep him in perfect peace, whose mind is stayed on thee: because he trusteth in thee."* You and only you can stop those negative thoughts from controlling your emotions and causing you to make decisions or actions that are contrary to the Word.

Is God worried about it?

Do you honestly believe that your heavenly Father worries about what you and I worry about? He does not worry, period! If He is not worried about it, why should YOU worry about it? Are you His child? His Word says that He cares for you! 1 Peter 5:7, "Casting all your care upon him; for He careth for you." Therefore, stop making excuses as to why you worry about things.

What you should be thinking about

Philippians 4:8 Finally, brethren, whatsoever things are true, whatsoever things are honest, whatsoever things are just, whatsoever things are pure, whatsoever things are lovely, whatsoever things are of good report; if there be any virtue, and if there be any praise, think on these things.

Colossians 3:2, "Set your affection on things above, not on things on the earth." In Greek, "to set your affection on something" means to *exercise the mind.*

Instead of exercising your mind on negative things and worrying over things you should not be worrying about, begin to do as God's Word says and start exercising your mind on positive things that build you up. Instead of looking at the problems in your life (sin, poverty, sickness, etc.), look at the solutions (forgiveness, blessings, healing, etc.) in Christ Jesus! The truth is yes, those problems may be presenting themselves in your life as overwhelming, but THE truth is God's Word….period!

Your thoughts
Let me ask you this... if you could take an inventory of the thoughts you have been thinking over the past week, what kind of thoughts were they?

- Were they mostly negative or focused on problems and cares of this world?
- Have they mostly been thoughts that tear you down and get/keep your eyes on the problem?
- Were they positive thoughts that have been building your spirit up?
- How much time have you been spending over the past week thinking about the goodness of God?
- How God is your healer, deliverer, provider, etc.?

Here are three things you need to do to renew your mind to God's Word:

1. STUDY: 2 Timothy 2:15 says, "Study to show thyself approved to God, a workman that needs not be ashamed, rightly dividing the word of Truth." I learned how to rightly divide God's truth when I attended Global Awakening School of Ministry and I was forever changed. The best way to know God's word is to study it. Go through the New Testament beginning in Romans and underline every verse that says, "in Christ," "in Him," or "in Whom," "By Christ," "Through Christ," "through Him." Pause at each mention and ask yourself, "How does this Reality change my perception of who I am?" What is God asking you to believe about yourself?" *(Who We Are In Christ, McIntyre, Joe)*

2. CONFESSION: Confess the Lordship of Christ over your life **daily**. Declare the truth of the Word; soon, it will become established in your heart and your life. Speak out who you are in Christ and what He has redeemed you from. Speak out His promises and blessings over your life. Spend time every day with Father and remind Him what His Word says about YOU. Create personal affirmations and speak them aloud daily when you look at yourself in the mirror. Dr. Randy Clark, Global Awakening College of Ministry, explains it like this: "*Confessing the Word of God cannot be approached as a "mechanical" thing but as* **a Father/Son-Daughter relationship** *and resting in the Father's promises. Faith will cause us to rest in the promises rather than strive and be anxious. Healing (Inner or physical) comes from "intimacy with God." Obedience brings healing. Out of intimacy, God speaks.*"

3. MEDITATION: This is not the meditation advocated by New Age groups, Eastern gurus, or yoga. NO!! Josh 1:8 says that "*this Book of the Law(the WORD) shall <u>not depart from your mouth</u>, but you shall <u>meditate</u> in it day and night that you may observe to do according to all that is written. For then, you will make your way prosperous and have success.*" T H E N… when? After you have meditated day and night and hidden that Word in your heart. The Hebrew meaning of meditate was to speak the Word over and over and over and over again—think of it like a cow that chews her cud- she chews it, swallows it- brings it back up, and chews and chews it again. (a gross example, yes, I know).

When you develop these three habits as lifestyles, you will grow in God. It may not be easy at first, but after a month or two, if you continue to do these things, you will notice a "life change"!

If your situation seems insurmountable right now- know that you are being *kissed with divine grace* to overcome what others would not or could not. We believe by faith that when you're done reading this book, you will defeat the worst damage of your past as long as you continue answering YES to His question, "Do you want to be made well?" This book helps provide inspiration and information to engage your inner healing and deliverance journey fully. God is so eagerly waiting to design beauty from your ashes. When He heals, delivers, and restores you, He does it with an exclamation point!! Remember that, and don't you ever forget it. Be encouraged!

Through your inner healing journey, you will realize that what beat others won't beat you!

Weekly Challenge and Amygdala Prayer

For the next few weeks while you're reading this book, find scriptures in God's Word to stand on by faith, meditate daily, and speak out loud. God will show you that He is faithful to His Word and cannot lie. He will do just what His Word said He will do! Do you accept the challenge?

Father God, I bless your name and declare that what the Bible teaches us about you is true. We declare that your very nature is love. Your love for us does not depend on our merit or favor. It is just who you are. Father, help me feel secure in your love. I declare your love breaks down my fear and worries about my health, my finances,
my relationships and my future.

Father God, I ask you to put your loving healing touch on my amygdala. Take the fearful emotions and negative memories that I may have stored in my brain and sanctify them. Any neurological patterns of fear and worry must now submit to your love!

Father, remove the lies that have led me to believe that I will always have fear and anxiety and that I cannot change. I declare that I am not too old to change; with your help, I will become a new person. In Jesus' powerful name I pray.
Amen

"IF YOUR HEART *believes* YOU ARE NOT GOOD ENOUGH TO BE *loved* BY GOD, THAT IS EXACTLY HOW YOU WILL *feel* EVEN IF YOUR MIND *knows* BETTER."

CHAPTER 3

YOU "CHOOSE" TO CONSTRUCT YOUR WALLS

Yes! You read that right– YOU CHOOSE! You are in this emotional mess because of choices you have made and beliefs you have held in your heart. You may have chosen to put up a wall that blocks you from receiving love because you have been hurt, and you believe that putting up that wall it will keep you safe from being hurt again. The reality is that it does not work. Your wall does not keep you from getting hurt- - it only keeps you from freely receiving love as God intended. Read that sentence again---> Your wall does NOT keep you from getting hurt; it only keeps you from receiving what God has intended for you to have.

It is only through receiving the love of God in your heart that you can be in that safe place that God intended you to be in. Two kinds of people need inner healing: sinners and victims. That pretty much takes in every single one of us. Once the sinner comes to Jesus and accepts Him as Lord and Savior, the sin problem is dealt with for eternity. The problem facing them now is the need for freedom from their sin's "present" effects. As far as the victim of another person's sin, Jesus paid special attention to those in His day. Those hurts stimulate reactions that, if not dealt with, eat away at the inner being of the wounded one in such a way that they cause many more problems than the original hurt. It is so important not to let your heart build those walls!!! I hope to help you tear down any walls you have built up from things done to you as a sinner- or as a victim.

Most addictions, for example, are rooted in your needing to be loved, not being fulfilled. Your capacity to receive love is hindered by the walls you constructed, which were meant to protect your heart but cause other problems. If Satan can keep your God-given needs from being met God's way, you become vulnerable to seeking out alternative ways to meet those needs. Sin is usually just a vain attempt to manage your emotional pain and lack of fulfillment.

Why do you lash out at somebody when they say the wrong thing? Because you are making them pay for what somebody else did to you. When you fail to love others, you sin because Jesus commands us to love one another. However, if your need to be loved is unmet because of the walls you have constructed in your heart, it will be difficult to love others. You cannot freely give something you are not receiving.

Do you want to live the life God intended for you to live and walk in?

Do you want to love others as Jesus commanded?

Then, you will need to work on the walls in your heart, preventing your need for love from being fulfilled. A heart that is not regularly receiving God's love is a heart that will not be emotionally healthy. Therefore, that person will be prone to struggle with sin as a vain attempt to meet their God-given needs to receive and experience His love. A former student in our inner healing class who dealt with an enormous amount of unforgiveness left the group because they refused to forgive people who had wronged them in their past. The question asked in class was, "Are you telling me I HAVE to forgive so-and-so for the horrible thing they did to me?" When we took them to the scripture Matthew 18:21-22, *Then Peter came to Jesus and asked, "Lord, how many times shall I forgive my brother or sister who sins against me? Up to seven times?" Jesus answered, "I tell you, not seven times, but seventy-seven times."* and told them we didn't say that, but the Word of God did. They got very upset and just walked out.

Here is the problem: You will not let down your walls because you believe your wall is doing something for you, i.e., protecting you from getting hurt. Until you deal with the wrong belief that your wall is "protecting you," it will be extremely difficult to let it go. Some people cannot let go of anger because they do not realize it is negatively impacting their lives, maybe even causing health-related issues.

The Holy Spirit is Your Counselor

The foundation of this type of ministry is based on these two important scriptures:

"But the Comforter [in newer translations, they call Him the Counselor], which is the Holy Ghost, whom the Father will send in my name, he shall teach you all things, and bring all things to your remembrance, whatsoever I have said unto you." John 14:26 KJV

"However, when he, the Spirit of truth, is come, he will guide you into all truth: for he shall not speak of himself but whatsoever he shall hear, that shall he speak, and he will shew you things to come." John 16:13 KJV

The focus of inner healing is to get you to a place where you can receive counsel directly from the Holy Spirit, who speaks to your heart and not just your head. While you can change what you logically believe, only the Holy Spirit can change what you experientially believe. Transforming the inner man does not once and for all fully reform your flesh this side of physical death, but rather, it slays ITS POWER TO CONTROL YOU while clothing you with the righteousness of Jesus. Another focus of Inner Healing and Freedom is to help you learn the 5 R's of dealing with any hurt:

1. **Recognize**
2. **Repent**
3. **Release**
4. **Reckon**
5. **Resurrect**

We use the 5 R's in almost every situation we deal with and minister to. The 5 R's are not a 1-2-3 step formula. There is a 6th R, which is the ultimate goal for Inner Healing - **Reconcile.** . An "exchange" and "change" happen when you experience the 6th step of reconciliation with God. The work of forgiveness and obedience that one experiences with the Holy Spirit changes your relationship with the Father for the better through a spiritual exchange.

The Role of Your Emotions

Often, you are told to "deny your emotions," that your emotions can lie, or that you cannot go by your feelings. I'm afraid I have to disagree! Emotions tell you what your heart believes to be true. If your heart believes you are not good enough to be loved by God, that is exactly how you will feel, even if your mind knows better. When a child is taught that it is unacceptable to cry or show or feel emotion, they are being taught to bury their pain, and that is extremely dangerous emotionally. We all need to be real about how we feel. You should never use your emotions to manipulate others, wear your feelings on your sleeves, or make others feel like they are walking on eggshells! You must be real about your feelings. True inner healing comes, then, not by making a broken thing good enough to work but by delivering you from the power of that broken thing so that it can no longer rule you and by teaching you to trust His righteousness to shine through that very thing.

When you heal by restoring just your self-image, it causes you to trust in something "repaired in the flesh," merely reshaping your old carnal practices, which leads you to failure. But the Lord heals by leaving the broken part right there and overcoming it by HIS nature. Your trust as a born-again Child of God can only be in HIS righteousness in you and for you--- always!

Denying your feelings will suppress your problems and hinder you from getting healed. You must know that feelings do not always speak the truth. You might "feel" guilty, but it does not mean you "are" guilty. Feelings often only tell you what is happening in your "thought life" and what you believe. Feelings are to alert you that something is wrong. If you begin to feel guilty, you need to get rid of the root of that problem and address it with the Word of God. (Again, renewing your mind!) Being balanced when dealing with your "feelings" is so important. It is not healthy for you to ignore those feelings, nor is it healthy to live by them. You will learn the scriptural way to deal with them.

Here's a little secret I want to let you in on. Your present pain is rarely IF EVER, rooted or caused by a present condition! Your present condition almost always triggers something you already believe about yourself or God because of past experiences. Emotional triggers are memories, objects, people, music, etc, that spark intense negative emotions. This change in emotions can be abrupt, and in most cases, it will feel more severe than what the trigger would logically call for.

When somebody triggers you, it is not them who is causing the pain you are experiencing, but more like they are "rubbing against a painful wound of your past." If your boss tells you that your work is not good enough, it will have little effect if you do not believe it. If your parents made you feel ashamed of a "B" on your report card as a kid, you might go through life believing that you are not good enough, and when somebody comes along and rubs that wound, it will be ten times more painful than if you did not have that "pre-existing belief" about yourself.

What if somebody calls you "stupid," yet you know you are not; their words will have little meaning. But if you already believe in your heart that you are stupid (even though you know in your head that you are not), and somebody comes along and speaks the lie, that will trigger you. You're trying to deny that awful perceived fact, and how dare someone tell you something that you are already struggling with.

God wants your ALL...wounds, pain, hurts, and sorrows included!

God desires to heal your wounds, take your pain and hurt from you, but you have to give it to Him. He carried your sorrows in His work on the Cross. In the Greek New Testament, "sorrow" refers to *anguish, affliction, grief, and pain.* God took all the world's sorrows, including yours, to the Cross and paid the price for them with His blood.

Isaiah 53:4: "Surely He hath borne our griefs and carried our sorrows, yet we did esteem him stricken, smitten of God and afflicted".

Psalm 147:3 He healeth the broken in heart and bindeth up their wounds.

You must release all of the hurt, and painful and fearful emotions into the hands of Jesus. Hanging on to fear, hurt, and pain **BLOCKS** the healing power of the Holy Spirit in your soul. Opening up and allowing Him to heal the wounds is vital.

In Matthew 11:28-29, The Lord says, "Come to me, all you who are weary and burdened, and I will give you rest. Take my yoke upon you and learn from me, for I am gentle and humble in heart, and you will find rest for your souls."

The above verse does not speak about a heavy physical burden but a burden in a person's soul because of the evidence in the later part of this passage, where it says, "YOU shall find REST unto your souls." Jesus is telling you to come unto Him and give Him your heavy burden and take His yoke, which is light and easy to bear.

Allow those painful emotions to be released as you give them to the Lord. It is okay to cry, sob, and let the damaged emotions come out as they are given to Him. Holding on to the pain and hurt will only prevent you from being healed. It is okay to sob or cry as the Holy Spirit reveals painful emotions that need to be released and how your heart needs to be healed. In no way does this signal you are empty on the inside, but quite the opposite!!

Realizing God's Love Opens your Heart to Receive Inner Healing

Knowing your heavenly Father's true nature will help you trust Him and open yourself up to receive the healing that only the Holy Spirit can provide.

Romans 8:32, "He that spared not his own Son, but delivered him up for us all, how shall he not with him also freely give us all things?"

God loves you not because of what you have done but because of who you are. The Bible tells us that while we were sinners, Christ died for us. He longed to have a relationship with you even before you became His child! Jesus waited so patiently because of His DEEP love for you.

Romans 5:8, "But God commended his love toward us, in that, while we were yet sinners, Christ died for us."

Jesus said that the greatest love a man can show for his friends is when he lays down his life for them. Jesus laid down His life for you – that is how valuable and dear you are to Him!

John 15:13, "Greater love hath no man than this, that a man lay down his life for his friends."

Did you know that God loves you with the same love that He had towards Jesus Himself? Read

John 17:23, "I in them, and thou in me, that they may be made perfect in one; and that the world may know that thou hast sent me, and hast loved them, as thou hast loved me."

You must learn of and realize your heavenly Father has agape love for you. Without knowing and taking hold of the love of God, you cannot be filled with His fullness:

Ephesians 3:17-19, "That Christ may dwell in your hearts by faith; that ye, being rooted and grounded in love, may be able to comprehend with all saints what is the breadth, and length, and depth, and height; And to know the love of Christ, which passeth knowledge, that ye might be filled with all the fullness of God. "

Realize God's Will for Your Mind and Receive It!

Let's look at Romans 12:2 in the Passion Translation. It says, *"Stop imitating the ideals and opinions of the culture around you, but be inwardly transformed by the Holy Spirit through a total reformation of how you think. This will empower you to discern God's will as you live a beautiful life, satisfying and perfect in his eyes."*

This is such a powerful scripture! A total reformation of how we think. Can we even do that? We can. If the things of this culture and this world are weighing you down, remove the distractions and dedicate time to meditate on the scriptures. It's not His Will that we succumb to all of the pressures and ways of this world, especially as we draw closer to the day of His appearance. What He does want is for us to put on blinders, like what they put on a horse, and take Him at His Word. We have to choose to believe or reform our thinking to what He says about us. Reform your thinking about your life, situations, memories, and even your past. Putting spiritual blinders on helps keep you from being distracted by all that is going on around you.

2 Timothy 1:7, "For God hath not given us the spirit of fear; but of power, and of love, and of a sound mind."

Abuse, trauma, hurt, unforgiveness, and pain are all works of the devil. Get that from your head into your soul. Jesus came to destroy the works of the devil and restore His children to the fullness He created them to fulfill. When Jesus was here on earth, He went about doing the will of the Father in heaven, and this included healing all who the devil oppressed: *Acts 10:38, "How God anointed Jesus of Nazareth with the Holy Ghost and with power: who went about doing good and healing **all** that were oppressed of the devil; for God was with him."*

Jesus' desire for you is to heal broken hearts and set those who have been bruised at liberty(set free):

Luke 4:18, "The Spirit of the Lord is upon me, because he hath anointed me to preach the gospel to the poor; he hath sent me to heal the brokenhearted, to preach deliverance to the captives, and recovering of sight to the blind, to set at liberty them that are bruised."

And lastly, but not least, God wants to restore your soul from all the damage that was done to you:

Psalms 23:3, "He restoreth my soul: he leadeth me in the paths of righteousness for his name's sake.

Decree and declare that today is the day you surrender and release it ALL unto Christ.

Prayer for Giving God My YES!

Holy Spirit, I am making a choice today and I give you my YES. I want to be made whole, but I am scared and I feel weak. Help me to see past my issues and look to the many rewards ahead. Give me solid reasons to finish my healing journey and never quit.

Take the lead, Holy Spirit, and lead me to inner healing and deliverance. Give me the strength and courage necessary to take that next step in Your will for me. In Jesus' Name, Amen. Let every yoke be broken and enable me to help others break yokes, too.

In Jesus' name, Amen.

"IF YOU WANT TO POSITION YOURSELF TO RECEIVE *Inner Healing,* YOU MUST BE IN THE RIGHT STANDING WITH *God.*"

CHAPTER 4

INNER HEALING AND PILLARS TO INNER HEALING

In Luke 4:18, Jesus declared that He is *uniquely anointed to bring healing to the broken places in people's hearts (soul wounds), to set captives free, and to lead prisoners into liberty.*

As mentioned in the beginning, Jesus brings restoration to people's lives. Inner Healing deals with *your* response to hurts, traumas, and memories from the past. These hurts and memories may affect your life in the form of bad memories, feelings of worthlessness and inferiority, fears and anxieties, rejection, the inability to feel loved and accepted, etc. They may come from such things as separation from a parent through illness, divorce, or death (which can be experienced as rejection) or the experiences of failure or lack. It can also come from such things as overwhelming fear, abuse, sexual abuse, and a family history of problems such as alcoholism, violence, or involvement in the occult, and any unresolved burden of guilt, church hurt, or father/mother wounds and even "in utero" (in the womb)wounds.

Some of the hurts come from the fact that we are living in a fallen, sinful world. Events happen in our lives, such as accidents, disease, poverty, and natural disasters, that are not of deliberate choice. Hurts can come from your own wrong choices and responses. Oftentimes, repressed memories are pushed below your conscious thinking, where they stay, and are felt in debilitating ways because you unconsciously forget. These memories can express themselves in your life as fear, anger, anxiety, resentment, self-hate, guilt, unforgiveness, an inability to trust, persistent irrational beliefs, etc. When you do not *admit* to your fear, anger, resentment, etc., and instead choose to *suppress* them, that does untold damage inside your heart (SPIRITUALLY and PHYSICALLY).

When suppression becomes a habit, that begins the construction of a "practiced habit," which in turn invites demonic access. Suppression would seem to be the opposite of constantly unleashing fear or anger and thus building habits of uncontrolled panic and rage, but in fact, both invite the demonic. The difference is that because fear and anger have been suppressed, you, the wounded heart, are feeding a volcano, and someday, that volcano will erupt into panic attacks, severe trauma, or even a tantrum. When you suppress the hurt so that you can cope, the memory is not dealt with, and it remains, eventually incapacitating you. The Good News is this: God wants and can deliver and heal you of fear, anger, and every emotional problem and demonic thing!

You need to know that there are some Christians who refuse to believe Christians would ever need inner healing or deliverance ministry because this was all taken care of through the finished work of Jesus. Yes, you read that sentence right! A well-known minister preaches this and emphatically believes this hypocrisy! They propose a similar philosophy: "We don't need to look at our past or what is wrong with us all the time. We don't need counselors or counseling. We only need to look at the Cross." Stepping into personal freedom is not that simple for many believers. I've seen this denial over and over. Denial of a problem will not heal you, and what you do not deal with will eventually deal with you and hinder you. Real freedom in Christ involves facing reality and overcoming it with the truth of God's Word. You must understand that you become more holy as you walk with the Holy One! People needing Inner Healing do not have the overall picture of what is happening inside them. You need to pray for the Holy Spirit to open your eyes so you can see things the way HE sees them inside of His children. Inner Healing brings wholeness to the inner being and sets you free.

The Inner Healing and Freedom's approach teaches:

- Various areas of emotional hurt and trauma
- How to identify such things as defense mechanisms, inner vows, unforgiveness, in utero wounds, inner vows, mother/father wounds, and so much more
- How to address issues with the presence of the Holy Spirit
- Spiritual discernment and knowledge of where ungodly beliefs, unhealthy expectancies, and tormenting judgments exist as a result of those emotional and mental wounds.

Prayers are provided for you throughout the book as these issues are addressed and exposed.

The late Dr. David Seamands, Methodist Theologian and pioneer in the inner healing movement says in his book Healing Damaged Emotions: "*There is something you need to understand, and that is that the gospel is most practical and gets right down to where you live. (I Cor. 2:2) As Americans, we have been weaned on indiscipline, indecency, and sensuality; we are living in modern Corinth. In our society, it is very difficult for anyone to grow to young adulthood without suffering some damage. There are scores of young men and women who were fed a lot of false and harmful ideas/information by well-meaning but ignorant parents, preachers, (and) authority figures. Now, they are unfit for marriage, unable to be husbands or wives who can live without fear, guilt, and shame. Damaged? Yes, badly. God has divine repairs and healing for you.* (Seamands, David, 1981, *Healing for Damaged Emotions*, Cook Publishing) If you desire to take your inner healing journey further, I encourage you to get his book on Amazon and have it in your library for studying.

These general Biblical principles **must** be followed throughout the process for you to receive fully your heart healing:

1. Face your problems squarely
2. Accept your responsibility in the matter
3. Ask YOURSELF if you WANT to be healed

4. Forgive everyone who is involved in your problem

5. Forgive YOURSELF

6. Ask the Holy Spirit to show you your REAL problem (root) and how you need to pray

Jesus demonstrated compassion toward people through his comprehensive ministry that included preaching, teaching, healing, and deliverance. Compassion is the emotion we should naturally expect to find most frequently attributed to Jesus. He accepted those that others rejected. He removed shame and defended their honor. He set people free from the influence of evil spirits. He exposed deception and showed people spiritual truth. Jesus not only did those things, but He also healed wounded hearts. Do not think of compassion as weakness! It is SO, not weakness.

Dr Seamands has a great explanation of inner Healing. He says it like this, "*There is a realm of problems that requires a special kind of prayer and a deeper level of healing by the Spirit. Somewhere between our sins, on the one hand, and our sickness, on the other, lies an area the Scripture calls "infirmities." We can explain this by an illustration from nature. If you visit the western United States, you will see the beautiful giant sequoia and redwood trees. In most of the parks, the naturalists can show you a cross-section of a great tree they have cut, and they will point out that the rings of the tree reveal the developmental history, year by year. There is a ring that represents a year when there was a terrible drought. There are a couple of rings from years when there was too much rain. Here is where the tree was struck by lightning. Here are some normal years of growth. This rung shows a forest fire that almost destroyed the tree. Here is another of savage blight and disease. All of this lies embedded in the heart of the tree, representing the autobiography of its growth.*

That is the way it is with us. Just a few thin layers beneath the protective bark- the concealing, protective mask- are the recorded rings of our lives. These are scars of ancient, painful hurts...as when a boy rushed downstairs one Christmas dawn and discovered in his Christmas stocking a dirty old rock, put there to punish him for some trivial boyhood naughtiness. This scar has eaten away at him, causing all kinds of interpersonal difficulties.

Understanding that salvation does not give instant emotional health, then we will understand an important insight into the doctrine of sanctification. It is impossible to know how "Christian" a person is, merely on the basis of his outward behavior. Isn't it true that "by their fruits you shall know them" Matthew 7:20? Yes, but it is also true that by their ROOTS, you shall understand and not judge them. There are certain areas of our lives that need special Healing by the Holy Spirit. Because they are not subject to ordinary prayer, discipline, and willpower, they need a special kind of understanding, an unlearning of past wrong programming, and a relearning and reprogramming transformation by the renewing of our minds. This is NOT done overnight." (Dr. David Seamands, Healing for Damaged Emotions, pages 12-14).

Have you ever met someone who was into extreme sin, became Born Again, and immediately felt called to the ministry? After having a rather lengthy meeting with a young man, but against the pastor's better judgment, this new Christian was put into a leadership position because he said all the right things, did all the right things, hung onto the pastor's coattails, and was eager to learn. He was in a "honeymoon stage." A few months later, something happened in this position that he did not like or know how to handle. Instead of going to the pastor, he decided to handle it himself from the wounded emotions of his past and made a mess of the situation.

The pastor brought him in and had a good "heart-to-heart" with him, and things seemed OK. A month or so goes by, and a similar situation happens, and again, the young man responds out of his wounds. Once again, they have another heart-to-heart. By now, the pastor wonders if he did the right thing, letting that young Christian have a leadership role considering his "mess-ups." Soon, people within the congregation came to the pastor, expressing their concerns. After much prayer, the pastor brought this young convert into his office, but this time, he informed him he was asking him to step down from his leadership position and to consent to being mentored by the pastor. This suggestion infuriated the young convert to no end. "Who does he think he is to remove me from my position and think I will be mentored by him?" So, the young convert rebels against all authority and leaves the church, but not without causing some deep emotional hurt to the pastor and his family.

By next Sunday, the young man is attending the church down the street, and within one month, he is on "staff" as an Associate Pastor. In just a few months, he is making the same mistakes there that he did at the previous church. He is still responding to situations with anger. At this point, Pastor A has contacted Pastor B, and they meet for coffee and compare notes. When Pastor B sees that the identical things are transpiring at his church that transpired at church A, he realizes he must do something before his church is ripped to shreds. Pastor B calls a meeting with the young convert to express his thoughts and concerns. He tells him he had met with Pastor A to check on a previous staff member and found out a lot about his past, including some pretty severe anger issues.

After the young man blew up and became violent in their meeting, the pastor fired him- right there on the spot. Even that came with a problem because this young man had access to all of the bank accounts in the church. I know both pastors in this story very well, and the young convert went on to split more churches before he finally got the Healing that he needed. He is no longer pastoring today, but he is doing life coaching.

The young man had deep emotional wounds from his past, and none of us understood what had transpired. His arrogance and pride are why the Bible teaches against allowing a novice to minister.

A church leader must not be a new believer because he might become proud, and the devil would cause him to fall. - 1 Timothy 3:6

Almost 35 years ago, we used to say people needed deliverance, but today, I can see they needed Inner Healing. If we had any teachings or knowledge about Inner Healing, this young man could have received healing from any ministry within the church. His walls, which he had built so carefully that no one would notice, could have been revealed immediately. The anger issues he dealt with were from his childhood and being hurt over and over again, so he felt like he had to hurt others. He was even abusive to his wife and baby. A vicious cycle, to say the least.

Inner Healing is all about tearing down those walls, getting rid of the roots from the past, and healing the heart. The walls are so carefully built to *protect you from the outside*, *from moving forward*, to *protect you from further hurt*, and walls for you *to hide behind*. Where do you feel the most comfortable when you are hurting inside? Most people would say, "hiding behind someone or something." Many people say they isolate themselves when they are hurting. When I had walked away from Jesus many years ago, I would isolate myself in my apartment for days. I wouldn't talk to anybody, I wouldn't answer any phone calls. I wouldn't shower or even eat. I would literally sit for days in front of the TV and not move. I was hurting inside and hid from the outside world so I wouldn't get hurt again. Pretty sad!

Let me say *again* that Inner Healing is recognizing the hurt and using prayer, the prophetic, and the Word of God to heal deep soul wounds and deep emotional wounds that are caused by TRAUMA or ABUSE. We can ask Him, through the work of Holy Spirit, to do the same things He did during His early ministry, including healing trauma in people's lives, dealing with deceptions that are holding people in bondage, setting people free from demonic oppression, freeing them from things that are blocking their spiritual growth and keeping them from bearing fruit to the glory of God, and so much more. The trauma people face can be physical abuse, verbal abuse, sexual abuse, physical pain, or any emotional pain that they cannot cope with. Inner Healing and Freedom helps you get to the deepest root of the pain from the trauma, helps you exchange lies for truth, close doors that were opened by events, heal the broken places of your heart, and help you heal permanently.

Many people deal with trauma or abuse by disconnecting from their surroundings, which can stop their trauma memories and lower fear, anxiety, and shame. It is disconnection and lack of continuity between thoughts, memories, surroundings, actions, or identity. They feel detached from their environment, people, or their bodies. Characteristics and effects of soul disassociation wounds: depression, emotional overreaction, lost time, voices, self-harm (cutting), suicidal thoughts or attempts, and emotional shutdown. The Psychiatric community has words for these wounds. They call it *bipolar, manic-depressive, DID (dissociative identity disorder), alternate personalities, MPD (multiple personality disorder)*, and *PTSD*, to name a few.

There is also a relationship between soul wounds and demons. Trauma or abuse can be an entry point for demons. If someone says they are *tormented* by anxiety, fear, guilt, anger, or any other emotions, there is a strong possibility they have deep soul wounds that are tormented by demons, or they are demonized. Certain things such as exposure to the occult, witchcraft, Ouija boards, Eightballs, seances, levitations, palm readers, psychics, tarot cards, consulting a medium or fortune teller, reading horoscopes, tea leaves, involving yourself with crystals, New Age, Freemasonry, Wicca, and the list goes on and on, blatantly violate the Scriptures, and open you up to those spirits. (Deut 18:9-14)

Why do people feel stuck in these emotional patterns, and why do they keep going around that mountain time after time? Dr. Lisa Winchell, well known Christian Psychologist and founder of His Image, Inc. and In His Image Institute of Counseling and Training , says, "...*some individuals do not move forward in their overcoming and victory despite their sincere desires and much work that they put into it. Trauma emotions create enough CHAOS and UNREST in the brain that when they apply truth to it, it just gets kicked out by the "trauma emotions" that are stuck in the brain. Emotional trauma damages the psychological being after an event that overwhelms the natural ability to cope. The brain science behind trauma is that when something produces intense emotion in a person, that emotional memory is stored in the amygdala (an almond-shaped mass of gray matter inside each cerebral hemisphere in our brain involved with experiencing emotions). It is responsible for perceiving anger, fear, sadness, and controlling aggression. The amygdala helps to store memories of events and emotions so that an individual may be able to recognize similar events in the future where it stays and continues to trigger the person anytime something is seen or happens around them that has ANY similarities to the original trauma that caused the wound--- good memories OR bad. The Bible calls this a* **stronghold***. A stronghold is a defensive structure. We have positive strongholds and negative strongholds. Negative strongholds are fueled by past painful emotions and lies the enemy feeds us that produce more fear and more fuel for the trauma. Negative strongholds then produce "hyper-vigilance": a state of increased alertness, extremely sensitive to surroundings, especially after PTSD and complex PTSD. This person can become uncharacteristically oversensitive, fearful, anxious, easily offended, on edge, and pressed to resolve anxieties and their effect on their relationships and lives." www.inhisimagecounseling.org*

Medically speaking, trauma is the physical damage that happens to an organ of the body as a result of an injury. How can you be sure that when you have a physical injury, the consequences are limited to just the physical? How can you be certain that other parts of you are not affected by the injury and, therefore, traumatized? Some of the physical symptoms dealt with are gallbladder problems, intestinal disorders, female problems and cancers, and emotions that are affected, especially in the areas of anger and fear.

Traumas come in many forms. Here are a few listed below:

1. Sexual assault
2. Accidents
3. War
4. Emotional and physical abuse
5. Death of a loved one
6. Bad choices

The Bible tells us in John 16:33 NLT, "*I have told you all this so that you may have peace in me. Here on earth, you will have MANY SORROWS. But take heart because I have overcome the world.* John 14:27 NLT also says, "*I am leaving you with a gift: PEACE OF MIND AND HEART. And the peace Jesus gives is a gift the WORLD cannot give… so do not be troubled or afraid.* Isaiah prophesied that one of the ministries of Jesus would be to "heal the brokenhearted." When you understand that the word "broken" means "shattered into separate pieces," your heart (which is your spirit and soul or inner being) has been shattered into pieces.

So how does someone whose brain is in hyper-vigilance(*increased alertness and extremely sensitive to their surroundings*) and constant triggers receive this peace?? How do they replace the negative strongholds/triggers with good ones? *THROUGH INNER HEALING.* In the past, therapists believed that it took years for an individual to heal from trauma—this is NOT true anymore. In these last days, I believe God has opened a "flood" of knowledge to the Body of Christ, and people are being healed-body, soul, and spirit.

I stress the importance of renewing your mind to the Word of God, speaking His Word daily, and choosing to believe what His Word says about you! The "Church" has been and is being trained by the Holy Spirit to bring Inner Healing to God's people by identifying and replacing the lies they have believed about themselves or God in the trauma by breaking spiritual bondages surrounding the trauma through inviting the Lord's healing presence in to bring His truth, healing, and victory over the trauma. This textbook will help lead you through forgiveness for those who should have warned and protected you from danger. The incidents that carry the worst trauma to the inner person are usually those that were deliberately caused by someone who should have been in a position of spiritual covering and protection. We speak love and encouragement into hearts, asking Jesus to begin to heal all of your inner pain- and we will ask for forgiveness of those who caused the trauma- whether by accidents, sexual or other things. When God heals the inside, you are free to receive His healing on the outside.

Mending Cracks in Your Soul

Your body becomes lacerated, bruised, or broken because of the force of an object on or in it, but the soul cracks due to *trauma and emotional overload.* A crack in your soul is often much more severe than an injury to your body. If not treated properly, it could result in a warped personality, much like a broken bone left untreated grows back crooked. Mending these cracks requires a two-part remedy. Like epoxy glue, this remedy has both a filler and a hardener. One without the other looks like it just might work and even may work for a short time- but when both are used correctly, the crack will be filled in and healed to the point of leaving "no scars." The Holy Spirit provides the initial action of identifying the place where your heart is injured and filling the crack with truth. Still, the Word held and confessed repeatedly is the hardener to complete your healing process.

The key to healing and mending cracks in your soul is for the Holy Spirit to take you back through past/repressed memories and show you what happened in the *spirit realm at the time of the trauma.* Seeing the truth in the spirit realm is called "opening the eyes of the heart (or spirit)." Ephesians 1:17-18 says, "*That the God of our Lord Jesus Christ, the Father of glory, may give YOU the spirit of wisdom and revelation in the knowledge of Him, the eyes of your understanding (heart) being enlightened."*

Healing an emotionally wounded person can be complicated, but the problem can be compounded by the fact that demons can enter into people at times of trauma. One of the most dysfunctional characters in the Bible is the madman of Gadara (Mark 5:1-5). Yes, those demons were a problem, but *how* they got in was the fundamental problem. Because the Gadarene man had a crack in his soul, it allowed the demons to come in, and consequently, this was the last item that needed to be fixed. The spiritual cracks in your soul can be fixed when you recognize the problem and go to the Word of God as your textbook for treatment.

When a receiver goes through an Inner Healing session, they must fill this new void with God's Word throughout their lives and every situation until their healing is manifested. Minister John Eckhardt says in his book *Faith, Deliverance and Healing (2017)* that *"prayers using the scriptures have <u>power against the enemy</u> when prayed because they are based in the supernatural power of the Word of God. Praying the WORD has tremendous power to heal and deliver people from all kinds of bondages. The Bible is a formidable spiritual weapon that will send the devil running out of people's lives. When you speak the Word of God in faith, the enemy WILL BACK OFF. There IS power in speaking God's Word OUT LOUD! There IS power in declaring the benefits of God over every part of your life. Unbelief BLOCKS Healing and deliverance. Faith RELEASES the healing anointing. When you have faith that you will be healed, you draw on the healing power of God."*

God created us with emotions, so it is wrong to try to become emotionless- to withdraw to a state in which nothing ever bothers us. A state where we are numb- disassociated. That is NOT what God wants.

Eckhardt continues by stating, *"Deliverance IS the children's bread (Matt 15:26). Areas that the demons can be involved in are the mind, emotions, will, appetite, (and) sexual character. They can dwell in different body areas, including the stomach, chest, back, head, eyes, glands, shoulders, and even organs."*

Here's something to think about: there is scientific proof that the physical issues mentioned above are connected to trauma, abuse, soul wounds, and repressed memories.

Position Yourself to be Healed

Having an aligned relationship with God, yourself, and others is vital when positioning yourself to receive Inner Healing. The late Dr. Henry Wright (1944-2019), President and Founder of Be in Health Global, pastor, author and an expert in the Inner Healing Ministry, breaks down three essential pillars necessary to position yourself to receive healing for emotional wounds.

Pillar 1. Have a 'Right' Relationship with God

For healing to occur, you *must* have a relationship with the Healer. We're not talking about being born again, but actively having a relationship with Jesus. It is important to have a 'love bond' with the Father! A 'love bond" with Father means you have a life-giving, loving relationship and a connection with Him. You go from the head to the heart as you deal with issues and problems. You are not afraid to share anything with your Heavenly Father because you know how much He loves you.

Many Christians have what we call a "religion with God," not a relationship. Religion seeks to earn its favor with God. In contrast, a relationship accepts what God's Word says about being made the righteousness of God through faith in Christ (see Romans 3:22). This does not mean that you can live like the world, as that is unacceptable for a member of the royal family in the kingdom of God. But it means that when you are living for Christ, placing your faith in Him, and honoring Him in your life, you need to stand on what God's Word tells you about how you are justified (made innocent, as if you have never sinned), forgiven your sins, and made right with Him (see Romans 3:24). Let God's Word sink into your hearts; your conscience is purged from dead works to serve the living God (see Hebrews 9:14), and that through the Blood you can have confidence to enter the holy of holies (see Hebrews 10:19). I said that earlier in one of the lessons, but let's look at it again: *Understand that you become more holy as you walk with the Holy One! (Not by works) People needing inner Healing do not have the overall picture of what is happening inside them. Pray for the Holy Spirit to open your eyes so you can see things the way HE sees them inside you.*

Religion is an Enemy of Inner Healing

Dead religion is a terrible plague that hinders the healing of many emotional wounds. Religion does not connect you with the healer (the Holy Spirit) but actually hinders His work in your life. Religion promotes fear, pride, and legalism; an enemy to the healing process. Dead religion creates an atmosphere where defense mechanisms thrive. Defense mechanisms, such as stubbornness and anger, are there to protect you from further harm, but at the same time, they actively hinder and even block the Holy Spirit's power from healing your wounds.

Fear and *unforgiveness* are the most popular glues that hold together defense mechanisms. Dead religion is fear-based, whereas relationship is faith and love-based. God's Word tells us that love casts out all fear (see 1 John 4:18). Many today are afraid of God because they believe He is disappointed or even angry with them to the point of not forgiving them. Believing this way further fosters dead religion and creates fear, which brings torment (see 1 John 4:18). How are you supposed to heal if you are in bondage to fear and torment? Through a genuine relationship (not religion), a LOVE BOND with God. Your fears will dissolve as you are made perfect in love (see 1 John 4:18).

Unforgiveness is selfish (God will forgive us of even the worst offenses, why can't we do the same?), and pride (that person wronged *ME*) is the result of not trusting God (to take care of that person for what they have done). Unforgiveness is incredibly destructive. You are commanded to forgive; if you do not, you sin against God. (I did not say it; HE did in Colossians 3:13). Love is the opposite of these things (see 1 Corinthians 13). Bitterness is a sin- if you cherish it, you refuse to forgive. If it is true that people do NOT deserve to be forgiven, then neither do you. Forgiveness is grace and mercy, NOT a question of if you deserve it! Jesus gives us grace and mercy while asking, "Will *YOU* give grace and mercy to others?"

As you allow God's deep and overflowing love and forgiveness toward you to sink into your heart, your unforgiveness towards others begins to dissolve instantaneously. It is, therefore, vital that you have a non-religious relationship with God to dissolve your defense mechanisms so that you can be healed emotionally. Overcoming the religious mindset is an especially crucial step to position yourself to receive healing for your damaged emotions. Religion will try to keep you from being healed. It will give you every religious excuse possible; therefore, you must be on guard.

Pillar 2. Have a 'Right' Relationship with Yourself

Self-hate is one of the most binding emotions in the ministry of deliverance and inner healing. It's hating the person in you that God has created and loves dearly. There is no doubt whatsoever that this is one of the *most destructive* plans of Satan against the children of God. The fact is that when you hate yourself, you are hating somebody that God made with His own hands, created in His image, and purchased with the redemptive blood of His dear Son. When you don't want to believe the truth, you protect it and live in a false reality. The way you get healed is to FACE the truth head-on- and bring it to Jesus. Beloved, HE already knows what is there- and there is nothing so awful about you that He does not already love. He loves the MESS. When you challenge what gives you SECURITY, you feel threatened inside- you get angry, and that's when the tormenting spirits have permission to come in.

I assure you that such hate opens you right up to tormenting evil spirits. Hate permits those spirits to act on your behalf against this person you hate, especially when an inner vow is made. Scores of *mental* and *physical infirmities* are rooted in self-hate. When you take on this attitude, you're hating God's special creation, and evil spirits will assuredly team up with you.

Having a right relationship with yourself is seeing yourself as God sees you and agreeing with His Word about the person He has made in you. It is not a prideful or arrogant way of seeing yourself but rather a humble and thankful expression of the great and wonderful person that God made in you. Being released from self-hate has an enormous effect on the healing process for many who are bound with various emotional and physical infirmities.

Pillar 3. Have a 'right' relationship with others

Are you out of relationship with others? Are you holding a grudge or failing to love others as Christ has loved you? Then you are not in right relationship with God either. Jesus warned us that if we do not forgive others from our hearts, our sins stand between us and the Father (see Matthew 6:15), but we also give legal grounds to tormenting spirits to operate in our lives (see Matthew 18:34-35).

For if ye forgive men their trespasses, your heavenly Father will also forgive you: But if ye forgive not men their trespasses, neither will your Father forgive your trespasses. Matthew 6:14-15

And his lord was wroth,(angry) and delivered him to the tormentors, till he should pay all that was due unto him. So likewise, shall my heavenly Father do also unto you, if ye from your hearts forgive not every one his brother their trespasses. Matthew 18:34-35

How can you expect to receive Inner Healing for your damaged emotions if you are away from God and you are in the territory of tormenting spirits? If you want to position yourself to receive Inner Healing, you must be in the right standing with God. Jesus tells us that if we forgive others, then we are forgiven (see Matthew 6:14). That is a promise!

Having your heart clean from ungodly feelings towards others is vital to healing your damaged emotions. The root of unforgiveness is a lack of trust in God. People hold so tightly to unforgiveness because they feel like *they are the only ones concerned about justice coming to that person who wronged them.* They do not believe that God will make sure that justice happens. There was someone who refused to forgive a person who had done so much wrong to them. Even when this person was encouraged with "*For if ye forgive men their trespasses, your Heavenly Father will also forgive you: But if ye forgive not men their trespasses, neither will your Father forgive your trespasses*" *Matthew 6:14-15* they refused and said they "were done" and walked out of our class.

Do you need to forgive someone (including yourself)?

Take this challenge:

1. The *resentment* challenge. Is there someone you resent and have never let off the hook? Parent, brother, sister, sweetheart, marriage partner, friend, coworker, teacher, someone who misused you sexually? Someone who hurt you so deeply or betrayed your trust?

2. The *responsibility* challenge. Have you ever said, "IF ONLY" my parents, spouse, children, life, or God had given me what they owed ME, etc? I would not be in THIS mess right now. I would not have these personality issues, etc. However, that's probably not true. I was guilty of saying that- but I had to take responsibility for my actions and my feelings and not use the "IF ONLY" card.

3. The *reminder and reaction* challenges are subtle. Have you ever reacted against someone because they remind you of someone else? Maybe you dislike how hubby disciplines your children because it reminds you of your dad and how he overdid discipline so that you may get snippy and resent him. After all, you have never fully forgiven your father, and your reaction to those reminders of that unforgiving person from the past triggers RESENTMENT. It is time to put it aside and lay it all down at the foot of the Cross. It is time to move on in life and do what God has called you to do. Without forgiveness, there can be no inner healing!

"IF YOU GOT THE *root*, YOU GOT THE *fruit*."

CHAPTER 5

BITTER ROOT JUDGMENTS, EXPECTANCIES, INNER VOWS, AND DEATH WISHES

What are Bitter Roots, Anyway?

Roots support plants and provide all the water and nutrients they need to grow. Similarly, we have roots that allow us to draw nurture from God, others, self, and nature. Those "roots" begin to grow from your first encounter with life and are well-developed by the time you are around 3 years old. It's the same way you learn accents in speech, the same way roots are practiced, hidden, automatic, and developed early in life. From these "roots," spring forth the trunk, branches, and leaves that make up who you are and how you respond to life. Those "roots" are affected by your environment while growing up. If your childhood was filled with nurturing love, gentle touches, and tender looks, you can draw good things into your life and produce good fruits. However, if you were exposed to an unsafe environment filled with strife, anger, hate, abuse, rejection, neglect, or abandonment, then your "bitter roots" will draw bad things from Satan and others, and you will produce bitter fruit in your life.

"If you've got the fruit, then you've got the root!" Plain and simple. If you have good roots, you drink nourishment from God and others, but if you have bitter roots, you drink poison from your hurtful bitterness. Roots that are contaminated with disease affect the entire body. Essentially, the root determines the fruit. You will never receive good fruit from a bad tree or root. You cannot kill a fruit tree just by picking the fruit off of it.

Under the right conditions, the same fruit will appear repeatedly, rearing its head in other areas of your life. Deliverance ministry is terrific, but it often does not get to the root issues that produce the bad fruit in a person's life. It is important to dig down and kill the root cause of the bad fruit, too. Even then, it may take several times to remove all of the strength from the bad root to put it to death finally. When we do an Inner Healing session, and there are deep roots to be dealt with, we, most times, have that person, as an act of obedience and faith, physically remove roots (whether from their head, their heart, or from the ground) calling their names out as they dig them up and get free from them. An enormous amount of healing has happened in doing it that way rather than just "saying" it aloud.

Bitter Root Judgements

Judgmental and critical spirits are some of your life's most destructive bitter root influences and can hinder your ability to receive and give love away. We often judge others as a result of being hurt or wounded by something that was said or done. The judgment can be bitterness, blame, condemnation, jealousy, envy, unrighteous anger, or unforgiveness. When you judge them, you set a spiritual law that demands a response in motion. The way you judge others is the way you will be judged. (Matt. 7:1-2) That is not something you want to experience! The standard and measure of your judgment will come back on you at some point throughout your life. Unfortunately, the judgment you receive is usually much more significant than what you sow because of the laws of sowing, reaping, and increasing. (Gal. 6:7, Lk. 6:38). It is not God judging you, but the law. When you judge somebody for the wrong done to you, you are demanding payment for those wrongs. You cannot expect mercy for yourself and judgment for others who wronged you because this is contrary to the Word of God. Your bitterness or resentment towards those who hurt you causes a judgment that demands justice. The judgment against you is the curse of reaping what you sowed.

Judgments have the full power of the law behind them (Matt. 7:1-2) and come back on you through your defilement of others around you. The judgment reinforces the ungodly beliefs and causes you to develop bitter expectations from the decisions.

Bitter Root Expectancies (BRE)

Bitter expectations are more psychological and affect your mind, but they can seem like the truth because of the fulfillment of the Law of Judgment. Most bitter root judgments remain hidden or forgotten until Holy Spirit brings them back to your remembrance. Bitterroot expectancies are the first indicator that you have these judgments as the fruits that come from them and appear in your life!

Below are examples of some bitter-rooted expectations we have all been guilty of as children of God — because after all, we live in a fallen world.

"He will never complete that task; he never, ever does!"
"There's no doubt about it; she'll be angry because she's always angry about that."
"They'll all reject me when I ask them." "All men are alike." "All women gossip," "I
will never marry again," and "I will never trust again."…

Bitterroot expectancies almost always come true. After all, you've never healed from BREs – meaning they will persist as self-fulfilling prophecies chiseled in stone because (for the most part) you do not even know that you are root-bound in a prison of bitter roots. In 2 Corinthians 10:4, it mentions *that strongholds are a part of the fortress of the flesh.* Someone once called it "Stinkin-Thinkin," a personal stronghold in your mind that keeps you bound with negative thoughts.

When dealing with judgments and strongholds, listen to every word you speak and ask yourself questions to find the diseased root causing the bitter fruit. When the words are spilling out, you need to understand that there is a good reason you are thinking that way, i.e., "stinkin-thinkin'." You may have tried repeatedly to overcome these judgments and realized you cannot or do not know how. In Inner Healing, we work towards finding the root cause for that way of thinking and deliverance from a poisoned mind.

Bitter roots are the result of your sinful reactions to hurt. Thus, critical, condemning judgments of people, refusal, or inability to forgive someone will defile you ---think about that for a moment. Instead of nourishment, your roots are swimming in poison. In childhood, when we judge and condemn a parent(s) for an actual or perceived wound, it will come out in life and adulthood by tempting people without bitter root expectancies.

"See to it that no one comes short of the grace of God; that no root of bitterness springing up causes trouble, and by it may be defiled." Hebrews 12:15.

Galatians 6:7 says, "...whatever a man sows, he will also reap."

How does the root of bitterness establish itself in the core of our being?

Here are some illustrations below:

1. A young child was molested, and it was never addressed. A Bitter-Root Expectancy was formed, and a resulting vow was made which they will carry for the rest of their life until the trauma is addressed. **Bitter Root Expectancy:** "I will always get hurt in love. **Vow:** "I will never enjoy intimacy when I get married."

2. Little one whom family members abused in many ways, and now at age 10, is being shamed by one of them by putting her wet panties around her neck and making her go out and play with the other kids. "That will teach you!" she is told. Yes, it did teach her. That moment taught her many damaging things, such as: "I am bad." "I will always be hurt by people who love me." *Can you find the bitter root?*

"The way we forgive we are forgiven," (Mk.11:26 & 2 Cor.2:10). "Fathers shall not be put to death for their children, nor children put to death for their fathers; each is to die for his own sin" (Deu. 24:16).

Two of the most important people you can forgive when forgiving others are your mother and father. A bitter-root judgment is a judgment that a person makes during childhood against their father, mother, caregiver, or relative. Many times, it is a subconscious judgment rather than a conscious one. It goes down deep into their heart, mind, and spirit.

A root of bitterness comes from unforgiveness and can lead to resentment that defiles others. It comes from failing to secure God's grace to forgive.

Hebrews 12:15 says,

"See to it that no one comes short of the grace of God; that no root of bitterness springing up causes trouble, and by it many be defiled . . ." (NASB)

Bitterroot judgments will cause you to become more like the one you judge. These judgments are rooted in the past and can influence your present and future. Then, because of the law of sowing and reaping and the law of judgment, the one who judges at some point in his life sentences himself to do the things he once felt about his parents.

Romans 2:1-2 says,

"Therefore, you are inexcusable, O man, whoever you are who judge, for in whatever you judge another you condemn yourself; for you who judge practice the same things. But we know that the judgment of God is according to truth against those who practice such things." (NKJV)

God Wants You to Honor, Not Judge Parents

You may have just read that title and thought, "I am done with this book!".... "nobody is going to tell me I need to honor my parents, no sir, not after what was done to me!" Just hold on and stay tuned to see where this is going! God has given us many laws throughout the Bible that influence our lives profoundly. Three of God's laws affect all of us. One of the laws in the Ten Commandments says,

"Honor your father and your mother, as the Lord your God commanded you, that your days may be prolonged and that it may go well with you in the land which the Lord your God gives you." (Deuteronomy 5:16 AMP).

God wants you to honor your parents, not judge them. Period! If we honor our parents, our lives will be long, and life will go well. Honoring our parents is a command with a promise.

The second law of judgment states that we will receive judgment or experience difficulty in the same areas of life where we have judged others.

Matthew 7:1-2 says,

"Do not judge and criticize and condemn others, so that you may not be judged and criticized and condemned yourselves. For just as you judge and criticize and condemn others, you will be judged, criticized, and condemned, and in accordance with the measure you use to deal out to others, it will be dealt out again to you." (AMP)

Bitterroot expectancies (**BRE**) tempt others to hurt you in the same way you were harmed in the past. It infects your mind and your heart with "bitter root expectancies."

When you judge your parents, you also dishonor them and put the law of dishonoring into motion. (Deut. 5:16). You put a curse on yourself, and soon you see that things are not going well for you.

When you judge, the bitter expectancies you form in your mind and spirit are drawn out by the people closest to you. For example, if a wife judged her father for being passive when she was younger, she would draw that passive nature out of her husband. If a man judged his mother for being overweight, he'd draw the tendency to be overweight out of his wife. She may not want to be overweight but she ends up that way and does not know why. If you judge your parents for getting a divorce, you will draw that same tendency out of your spouse towards divorce.

Identifying Bitter-Roots

Look for patterns or habits you know in your own life that have brought you *fear, doubt, rejection, heartache, jealousy, or anger*. These patterns may be from judgments you have made against your mother or father. Notice situations where you repeat the same behavior over and over. "In an interview in *Christianity Today*, a man told the interviewer: *"The first time that I made a list of my bitter-root judgments against my parents, it took me three weeks. I was reluctant to make the list because I felt that making the list was disloyal. However, I was not looking for my bitterroots to judge my parents. I was looking for my bitter roots to take responsibility for my sinful judgments".*

You may have difficulty seeing your bitter-root judgments. Pray and ask God to reveal the judgments that you have made against your parents. Please make a list of them. It may take some time. God will reveal what you need to know at the appointed time when you need to know it.

Focus on Habits or Patterns

As you look at your list of bitter-root judgments, focus on habits or patterns that you have noticed that have repeatedly brought you frustration, heartache, grief, or unforgiveness. Do you repeat patterns of behavior that are damaging to you or others? Sometimes, I refer to it as "going around that mountain again!". How often have you confessed your sinful behavior to God and asked forgiveness? Do you continue to repeat the behavior no matter how much you confess it and pray to be set free from it? Why should YOU repent after people hurt YOU so severely? The law of sowing and reaping takes place here. Whatever you sow, you will undoubtedly reap. No matter how it hurts, it is essential to do the Godly thing and forgive.

Some examples of bitterroots that can indicate judgment toward your parents include perfectionism, addictions, critical spirit, emotionally unavailable, hostility, manipulation, working continually, rejection, uncontrolled anger or rage, bitterness, or performance orientation.

Canceling a Bitter-Root Judgment with the 5 R's

There are nine steps to cancel a bitter-root judgment, but you can't do this without the 5 R's. The 5 R's are essential in coming out of agreement with this root that's been keeping you in bondage for years.

1. First, you should *recognize* that the sinful pattern of having bitter roots has affected you and others. Confess your bitter-root judgment. Name whom you judged and for what you judged them.

2. **Repent** and ask for forgiveness, forgive yourself, and repent and renounce your sin, which means to fall out of agreement with it.

3. Ask God to nail your *sin of judgment* to the Cross. (Colossians 2:13-14)

4. Allow yourself to grieve any feelings of pain or loss and release them to God.

5. **Release** forgiveness and ask God to remove any unforgiveness or other sins from your heart and replace them with the opposite of those sins.

6. **Reckon** as dead the bitter root and then ask God to give you a new heart by faith. (Ezekiel 36:26)

7. Ask God to meet the needs that were not met in you as a child. Some basic needs for adults and children are unconditional love, acceptance, worth and value, security, recognition, nurture, emotional nourishment, and comfort.

8. Ask God how this bitter root has affected your relationships with others. Pray for God to heal those relationships.

9. Thank Him for your answered prayers and for **resurrecting** you to be the person He created you to be. (Philippians 4:6)

Breaking the Power of Bitter-Root Judgments

As you work through the nine steps to cancel a bitter-root judgment, you are letting go of the past and asking God to lay the axe to the roots of your bitter judgments. It is a *daily discipline*. Stay encouraged even when feelings, emotions, and thoughts want to rear their ugly head. Just remember, I Corinthians 15:31 says that you die daily. When you are tempted to fall back into the old feelings, remind God what His Word promised it would do!

Matthew 3:10, *"And already the axe of God's judgment is swinging toward the root of the trees; therefore, every tree that does not bear good fruit is cut down and thrown into the fire."* (AMP)

The benefits of breaking the power of bitter-root judgments are love, joy, peace, freedom, forgiveness, grace, mercy, possibilities for restoration, new beginnings, and physical healing.

Forgiving through the Generations

Finally, many blessings and advantages come from forgiving through the generations. You can help restore broken relationships in your family. You can repair the destruction of many generations. You can help heal some of your family's wounds. As you confess and repent of your sins, you can break the chains of past generations. Freedom from the chains of the past will allow you and your family to live in the present and look forward to the future. Be part of rebuilding the ruined relationships through the judgments and sins in your family.

Isaiah 61:4 says: *"Then they will rebuild the ancient ruins, they will raise up the former devastations; And they will repair the ruined cities, The desolations of many generations."* (NASB)

What are inner vows?

God takes vows very seriously! (Take marriage vows, for instance!) (Num 30:2, Deut 23:21, Ecc. 5:4). Another bitter root that can arise from judging others is inner vows. An inner vow is a "hateful order" against your body, usually spoken as a child, that is sent through the heart and mind to the body. Those words that were said are a creative force that will happen to affect you until it is broken through the Cross. You do not grow "out of them" as you mature or have a change of heart. Your mind may forget them, but those vows will eventually manifest in your life and physical body. Even your good vows compelled by the flesh and not the Spirit will need to be released so your flesh does not rule in that area.

Exposing Dormant Vows

The manifestation of inner vows will lie dormant for many years until the time set by the vow or the right situation or person(s) triggers the vow to be activated. They are often forgotten until Holy Spirit reveals them to us. They lodge in your heart and cannot be removed by your own fleshly effort. They strongly resist change and will work in tandem with other bitter roots, hidden resentment, and fear. Only by using the authority of the Name of Jesus, usually by another believer, can a person be released from an inner vow.

Inner vows can block God's plan for your life. For example, most boys learn early that their mothers are very observant and remember almost everything they say or do (good or bad), especially related to emotions and feelings. Mothers use this knowledge later as a means of control. "You used to get excited about_____." "I remember when you liked to_____". A boy, under this pressure, may vow, "I will never show my emotions or feelings around a woman. It is not safe." Later when he is married, he may find it hard to express his feelings or emotions to his wife, even though he may want to share them. (They may have had good communication while dating, but *the marriage trigger* brings out the inner vow, and he now finds it hard as a husband.) Even though he wants to work things out, something inside that he is unaware of stops him. He may repent and try repeatedly, only to revert to the old pattern programmed by the *inner vow against his mother*. The inner vow will continue to confine him to isolation until it is broken in his life.

Inner vows can form complex structures of other bitter roots that must also be broken to be set entirely free. Let's look at the above example again: The son may have withdrawn from relationships, hardened his heart, and developed evasive and defensive habits to protect himself from hurt. Not only are there some bitter root expectancies and fears, but he may be incapable of trusting and probably has controlling actions such as fear. It is essential to understand that breaking free from all of these may take some time through an inner healing session, love, and forgiveness. Fears may be rooted in inner vows.

After an embarrassing or scary event, you may have vowed never to take any risks beyond your control, never to speak in public, never to grow up, never to try again, or never to wear hand-me-downs. You probably vowed, "I will never be unprepared when people ask me a question." You can be tense in group discussions, or if there are too many situations that require many quick adjustments, you may experience a mental breakdown or panic attack. *Can you relate?* I certainly can. Some of the most destructive vows concern personal relationships, especially marital relationships, and are rooted in a child's determination against his parents. If you said, "I'll get even with my mother or sister if it's the last thing I do," you may become angry at women, especially your wife or daughters (or vice versa for women). "I'll never let my brother or sister get the best of me again " may result in you becoming competitive in business or with peers and family. Or, you may vow, "I will never get angry like that," only to find yourself withholding anger until some situation causes you to explode like a volcano.

An inner vow is another type of bitterroot, a promise or determination to keep yourself from being hurt again. These are made early in life. Leviticus 5:4 tells us that a vow (or an oath) is a legally binding contract. It's a personal stronghold of the flesh and how you guard yourself from pain. (2 Cor 10:4; Prov. 4:23 and Ps 8:2,3) An inner vow can also be an idol you rely on instead of God by relying on your strength. An inner vow is preceded by words like *"I will," "I will never," "I won't," and "I will always."*

Some examples of inner vows:

1. I will never get angry.
2. I will never trust anyone again.
3. I will never cry.
4. I will always be strong.
5. I will do everything perfectly.
6. I will never let another man hurt me ever again.

A foundational lie is what you believe, a bitter root judgment is how you judge, a bitter root expectancy is what you expect, and an inner vow is a promise to protect YOU from further hurt.

Traits of Inner Vows:

   a. They are common to every individual

b. Sometimes, they are spoken, but more often *unspoken*. (As a man thinketh in his heart, so is he!)

c. They are powerful! Inner vows command you to think, act, and only feel as instructed.

d. Refuse to change without repentance.

e. They take on a life of their own.

Watch for any vows that start with, "I will NEVER do/say...."

When you repent of an inner vow, you must also repent of the habits you used to fulfill them. For instance, an inner vow to withdraw is fulfilled through watching TV, isolation, refusing to talk, immersing yourself in social media, and other distractions. An inner vow to not feel can be fulfilled through addictions, denial, or avoiding relationships. Galatians 3:3 says you must die to all inner vows, whether good or bad. The *cumulative effect* of bitter root judgments, foundations, lies, and inner vows is that when you use these to protect your heart, you rely on your own strength. You quickly develop a <u>heart of stone</u> that shuts out God, others, and yourself.

The Book of Hebrews clearly states that the bitter root will one day sprout, and when it does, "many will become defiled. " If that bitter root keeps growing, you will reap a harvest of pain for yourself and others. Bitterness is a weedy sin that will burrow into your heart, and you cannot stop the behaviors it causes. It is not one of those big, flashy sins- you cannot see it growing above the surface. It does not show itself like anger does or produce a rotten crop like disobedience. No, bitterness grows beneath the surface, down deep in the soil of your heart.

You can be particularly good at hiding it for a while. See, emotions progress. If the bitterness is not dealt with, it will progress to wrath or extreme anger. Then, if you do not deal with the anger, you begin to demand to get your way. If that does not work, you begin to talk negatively about the object of your bitterness in hopes of recruiting others for your team- to agree with you and justify your feelings. That is *slander*.

If all of the above goes unchecked, you will eventually have a desire to cause harm to the object of your extreme bitterness. If THAT is not addressed, people will be hurt, relationships can be destroyed, joy will be stolen, and any growth of the fruit of the spirit will be stunted!

Death Wishes

Death wishes are words that we speak *against ourselves* concerning death, such as, "I wish that I was never born." "I wish the Lord would just take me home right now." "I'm so embarrassed that I could just die." If there were difficult times surrounding the time you were in the womb, your birth, or just after birth, your mother might have made death wishes without even being aware of doing it because she felt that the world was not a safe place.

Defilement Lies Behind Death Wishes

The spirit that comes to earth to inhabit a new human being at conception has only the remembrance of the beauty and wholeness of heaven. If the parents love and long for the child to come, the child begins to recover from the shock of entering this world of sin and chaos. However, if the atmosphere outside of the womb is one of turmoil, fear, fighting, hurtful emotions, and violence, or if the delivery is difficult, then the spirit inside the child feels like this is not a safe place to live and begins wishing they were dead so they would not have to live their life in such a place. Death wishes may come if there were tragedies, deaths, or other traumatic happenings during the pregnancy or shortly after birth or if other children in the family were jealous of the new baby or did not welcome it into the family. Your parents may be disappointed that you were the "wrong" sex.

These death wishes show up in the new babies and young children as behavioral problems, self-hatred, chronic illnesses, dangerous physical conditions, or diseases, or they are accident-prone. The immune system does not work right because the body does not want to live. Death wishes can affect coordination and confidence or take the zest for life out of us.

Our Parents' Words Can Impact Us

The words from your parents can also cause a person to form death wishes. If you were told, "You are no good. You will never amount to anything.

You are hopelessly stupid, or I wish you were never born" you can begin hating yourself and wish that you were never born. We had a gal take our class and she shared with us that her father told her that the darkest day of his life was the *day she was born*. If you just felt like you were in the way or were an inconvenience to your parents, you may wish that you could die so the pain would go away. You may not have been conceived at a good time in your parent's life, and they may have considered having an abortion. If you were abused as a child, abandoned, given up for adoption, or rejected by your parents, you may feel like you do not have a right to live. You may wish that the Lord would just come, and you could be done with the miserable life here on earth and go to a better place.

Death Wishes Can Affect Your Physical Bodies

You can walk with a deliberate bent-over look that does not allow your body to move smoothly. It may affect your voice and rob the diaphragm of power to sing with gusto and joy. The person may not view life as more than just existing as long as they have to be here.

Death wishes may affect your sexual fulfillment. You engage in sex more out of duty or for whatever little enjoyment you may get from it. You never come alive to experience the glorious union with your mate in the spirit and ravish the love and joy of true sexual fulfillment. Usually, people with hidden death wishes do not even want to engage in sexual activities.

Hidden death wishes may also hinder one from fully expressing the talents and calling given to them by God. Their spirit is not free to venture and explore life.

You Are Probably Angry With God

Everyone who has hidden death wishes is angry with God deep within their spirit. You are angry with God for putting you in this messed up situation or for not being there when you needed Him in the womb. God was there and did not plan for your parents to respond to you the way they did. His plan was for good and not evil. (Jer. 29:11)

You may be angry at God because of the way you look. The degree to which you do not love yourself is the degree to which you are angry at God. Be careful of the words you speak over yourself because of how you look, for example, your facial features, body, height, and even weight. It is crucial not to say words of death but words of life. If you do not love yourself, you dishonor God, for He created you. Mark 12:31 commands us to love ourselves.

I have talked with some people who think they need to forgive God, even though **He** never did anything wrong. You need to be reconciled to Him in your heart. (2 Cor. 5:18-20) It would be best if you were open and honest with yourself. You must break free from the fear and shame of your past and confess your sins. Confession is like becoming a child again, open, vulnerable, and trusting. (Luke 18:17) As the shame melts away in this new transparency, you can begin to love yourself.

Repentance Starts Here

When you repent, you're telling God that you received a divine understanding of your behavior, and now you're ready to change, turn away from the wickedness, and begin a new relationship with God (Ezekiel 18:30-31; Acts 20:21).

You must repent for rebelling against being born where He put you and the family He gave you. Also, repent for rejecting yourself. Accept your body and ask God to reconcile you to your time, place, and position on this earth.

You cannot do this alone. God has assigned sons and daughters to Inner Healing and Freedom, who will pray with you to ask Jesus to woo the inner child within you to life and break the vows against wanting to be alive. Have them command the spirit, mind, and body to work in harmony.

Then rejoice! Be free and live to enjoy life and fellowship with God. Discipline yourself to choose life and blessing, not death and cursing daily. (Deut. 30:19)

Prayer For Bitter Roots Judgements and Expectancies

In the Name of Jesus Christ, I confess and repent of all my bitter-root judgments and bitter-root expectancies toward my father, mother myself, and all other persons, including those I remember and those I do not remember. I especially repent of those bitter-root judgments formed against parts of myself. I cancel all of them and destroy them by the Finger of the Living GOD, including all curses and effects. I bless all those judged with every blessing from the LORD, setting them free from all my judgments and condemnations in the Name of Messiah Jesus Christ.

I choose to honor my father and mother to the extent GOD's Will permits — in every area of my life. I repent and cancel all inner vows I have ever made contrary to the Will of my Heavenly FATHER. I destroy the curses and effects, replacing them with those that bless all involved.

I bring to the Cross for crucifixion all attitudes, habits, practices, and consequences coming from all of the above, reckoning them as dead on the Cross when Messiah died. I choose to hate all my sins enough to give them up through the Messiah, Who strengthens me.

I confess and repent of all wrongful judging from an impure heart involving blame, condemnation, anger, envy, jealousy, bitterness, and all wicked motives. I replace them with all the blessings I can give in the Name of Jesus Christ. I especially forgive all wrongful judgments coming against me.

I ask GOD to forgive me wherever I have sown wrongful thoughts, words, and actions and to spare me through Your Grace from reaping the effects of my judgments.

I forgive my father, mother, myself, and all others. I ask that the Holy Spirit bring anything I am unaware of in my mind. I pray for GOD's Richest Blessing on all who have wronged me.

I cancel all parental inversion that has taken place in my life and all bondage to performance orientation. I repent of and cancel all my sinful attitudes and practices not included in the above.

I replace them with the Love of GOD and His Holy Will for all and myself involved. Anything not included in the above that should be, I do now include in the Name of Jesus Christ of Nazareth.

I ask the Holy Spirit to complete anything not prayed correctly as necessary in the Name of Jesus Christ, in whose Name all of this is done for the Honor and Glory of GOD. I ask You, Jesus Christ, to come here now and take all the aspects of myself into Your Loving Arms.

I ask You to show me the lies that I have believed regarding any sins done to me or which I have chosen to commit.

I ask You, my Heavenly FATHER, to replace these lies with truth, giving forgiveness, cleansing, healing, comfort, and full, complete, and permanent deliverance from both the lies I have believed and any and all grounds given to Satan or his demonic forces. Fully redeem all the above failures and keep me from repeating the same. **Thank You, Jesus,** *AMEN*

Prayer To Cancel The Power Of An Inner Vow

Lord Jesus, I renounce the inner vow (name specifically) and how I have fulfilled them (name them). I ask you to forgive me for relying on this inner vow.

I forgive _____ for tempting me to make it. Forgive me for judging them.

Lord Jesus, by your power and authority, I ask you to nail this inner vow to your Cross along with all the ways I have fulfilled it.

I speak to my body, heart, mind, and spirit to no longer obey this inner vow. Lord, bring me new life where this inner vow once brought death. **In Jesus Mighty Name. Amen**

Forgiving OTHERS CAN BE EXTREMELY *hard*, BUT *breaking* OUT OF THE *bondage* IT HAS BROUGHT YOU UNDER IS *essential.*

CHAPTER 6

INNER HEALING THROUGH FORGIVENESS AND EXTENDING FORGIVENESS

And grieve not the Holy Spirit of God...Let all bitterness, and wrath, and anger, and another, tenderhearted, forgiving one another, even as God for Christ's sake hath forgiven you.
Ephesians 4:30-32

Judge not, and ye shall not be judged; condemn not, and ye shall not be condemned; forgive, and ye shall be forgiven.
Luke 6:37

Forgiveness is the mother lode to all inner healing!

Holy Spirit grieves over our grumbling, complaining, lack of kindness, and not forgiving others from the heart. You are sowing negative seeds by judging, condemning, and not being willing to forgive. Holy Spirit is grieved because He loves each of us so intensely, and He knows the significant harm that will come into your lives and the lives of our loved ones from negative seeds of unforgiveness. Judging, condemning, complaining, and unforgiveness are all intertwined. They are related to each other. They all indicate a *lack of forgiveness*. As long as you remain unrepentant of a bitter root, your response to an emotional stimulus will illustrate the law of sowing and reaping. This law operates legally. Jesus even went as far as to highlight the importance of forgiveness throughout His teachings. He even went as far as to say that if you are not willing to forgive others for what they did to you, then your Father in Heaven will NOT forgive you for what you have done. (Matthew 6:15)

What harm can come from such a negative sowing of unforgiveness? Damaged health, broken marriages, ruined relationships with children, with other Christians, and with fellow employees are just some of the harmful effects. Since forgiveness and the release of bitterness and hatred that it brings about are so important, you must learn what true forgiveness is, what it is not, and how you can effectively forgive. "*The laws of sowing and reaping and of increase ensure that all of your human relationships, because of your continually sinning flesh, must be ever accelerating to war and destruction. Nothing can stop that swing, save the cross of Jesus. That is the centrality of forgiveness: Heb. 9:22. Unless sinful propensities born of bitter roots are repented of stimulus demands response, and seed sown requires reaping; therefore, every hatred requires blood. The blood of forgiveness is central even to the possibility of continuance of human life.*" (*Transforming the Inner Man,* John & Paula Sandford pg. 98-99). When people finally realize how important forgiveness is and understand the significance of Jesus' words, they will want to forgive even their abusers, realizing that the abuser's behavior is usually a result of the way they have been treated. The battle with your emotions begins once the *decision* to forgive is made. I have seen it happen with my own eyes. The spiritual climate over you will change when you forgive. The unseen world is altered when you do something that agrees with Heaven! Angels are activated, demons are bound, and there is a shift in the atmosphere that cannot always be seen with the naked eye. Healing is released in the body, division among people becomes mended, and Heaven's favor is restored. It enables you to move on with your life instead of keeping some areas on hold until someone apologizes or some event happens to fix the pain. You do not have to stay imprisoned or stuck because of bitterness and unforgiveness. When you choose to forgive, you're released from the punishment of bitterness and can move on to rebuild your life. Because forgiveness is for you, you will reap the benefits.

Unforgiveness stifles God's destiny in your life. It clouds your motive. It pollutes your purpose. It tempts you to deviate from your course. You find yourself weighed down and easily worn out when unforgiveness is present. Working through the pain of feelings that have been damaged by the abuse and deep hurts of others is not easy. When you finally understand how necessary it is to forgive but find it impossible to make that choice, you must ask yourself whether or not there is a "spirit of unforgiveness" or "bitterness" holding you in bondage. If so, this is where deliverance plays a highly crucial role.

Let's go over that again! Forgiving those who have injured or abused you is a *requirement* for healing to take place. (I didn't say it; Jesus did). Unforgiveness, bitterness, and resentment are among the evil spirits that dwell in you when you stubbornly refuse to forgive over some time. Without any doubt, you need Jesus' power to forgive since it is far beyond your human ability, especially if the wounds are deep and they have permanently impaired your life.

When taking someone through an inner healing session, 99.999% of the time, it is unforgiveness that our recipients are dealing with. We will ask them if they are ready to "choose" forgiveness. We do not rush them! For some who have had deep-seated unforgiveness for a long time, we let them choose their own pace. When we lead them in prayer, they usually respond something like this:

"I CHOOSE to forgive _____

for _____.

I renounce the lie that _____

and I replace it with the truth _____."

Deciding to forgive is the first step. Some have been able to choose to forgive, but for others, the pain was so intense and so deep that they could not forgive. Forgiving is not just empty words—when you have a heart willing to forgive, the weights that hinder you are gone. When you forgive, you live in freedom.

What Forgiveness Is Not

1. Forgiveness is not a weakness but a strength.

2. Forgiveness does not restore trust but opens the door to the possibility of reestablishing such trust. Forgiveness is a gift. Trust must be earned.

3. Forgiveness often does not include restoring a relationship, friendship, or marriage. Forgiving your divorced or separated spouse, ex-prayer partner, ex-boss, or ex-pastor would be best, but the relationship often will not be restored. It's ok!

4. Forgiveness is not condoning sin or saying what was done is okay. If a person has sinned against you and God, they are guilty and must answer to God. He has said:

Dearly beloved, avenge not yourselves, but rather give place unto wrath: for it is written, Vengeance is mine; I will repay, saith the Lord.
Romans 12:19

Okay, so tell me… What Is Forgiveness?

Forgiveness is releasing a person from a debt owed to you. You give up your right to get revenge for the wrong someone has done to you. You lose your desire to "get even." It is a choice! In the New Testament, the dispensation of grace, we are commanded to turn the other cheek, go the extra mile, and bless our enemies. Jesus instructed us:

But I say unto you, Love your enemies, bless them that curse you, do good to them that hate you, and pray for them which despitefully use you, and persecute you. (Matthew 5:44)

If you can develop a lifestyle of praying blessings for those who hurt, disappoint, and reject you instead of criticizing and complaining, your life will be blessed. You will live in joy, peace, and love.

Have You Forgiven?

Have you forgiven your parents for your childhood hurts? Have you forgiven your enemies, friends, and loved ones who have hurt you so deeply? Many of you may have forgiven in your minds but only partially from your hearts. The poison of bitterness toward others must be drained from your inner man through inner healing. Then, the forgiveness will be complete. Otherwise, the negative reaping from unforgiveness and bitterness will defile your lives and the lives of those you most love. Every relationship in your life will be negatively affected. The very ones you most want to love and bless, you'll end up hurting the most. Let me ask you this: What is your offender doing right now? Do you think your offender is bothered by what they did or said to you? Do you believe that "your" unforgiveness is disturbing them? Is it possible that your bitterness and unforgiveness are inflicting pain on them, causing them to suffer, and paying them back for what they did? I can tell you the answer to these questions is definitely NO.

So why do you continue to hold unforgiveness in your heart? WHY?

What Do You Gain from Forgiveness?

1. Frees you from anger, resentments, and bitterness; brings you inner peace.

2. Helps your relationship with God and with others. His Glorious Presence increases.

3. It frees God to forgive your sins and answer your prayers!

4. Forgiving your parents is part of honoring your parents, which is the most significant key to marital harmony.

5. Your prayer power is no longer weakened. Mark 11:25.

What Is Unforgiveness?

Unforgiveness is a form of hate against another person. If a person hates somebody, it is a sign that they lack love in their heart. Why? They are not firmly rooted and grounded in the love of Christ, and Christ's love is not flowing through them. As simple as that sounds, that is how it works.

What somebody may have done against you is one thing, but if you take Satan's bait of unforgiveness to heart, it will do much more harm than they did. Do you want to continue to allow *their mess* to trouble you even more? Have they not done enough damage? Allowing yourself to hang onto hard feelings and become bitter is only causing your wounds to become even more infected spiritually.

Honestly, tell yourself (and look at yourself in the mirror and say this aloud), "*What good is it doing you to hold onto the hurt and bitterness that the enemy has tried to plant within you? It is doing nothing but harm and is holding you in bondage spiritually. The only reason you are holding onto those feelings is because it feels good inside!* Do not let this fool you; remember, we stated earlier that bitterness is known as spiritual poison.

The reason Satan wants you to hold onto that bitterness is to poison your soul. Jesus said that the devil came to steal, kill, and destroy. Satan wants to do just that to you. No wonder Satan makes unforgiveness "feel good"...he wants your soul to be poisoned! I love the British murder mysteries that occurred in the 1920's-1950's. The most common form of murder was cyanide poisoning. Most of the time, it was put in their tea. There is no foul smell but only the delightful aroma of almonds. There is no taste, but within seconds, at the most, minutes, you are dead. That is the same way the enemy of your soul is. He covers things up, he hides, he makes you think everything is OK, and you drink his tea over and over, and soon your soul is poisoned.

The poison of drinking unforgiveness and bitterness also blocks your prayer for physical healing and, in many cases, causes physical ailments. Did you know that buried resentments can cause arthritis and cancer? If you are dealing with some health-related issues, examine your heart to see if there is unforgiveness there. If so, who do you need to forgive?

The Steep Price of Unforgiveness

Unforgiveness is similar to a wound left untreated and has festered into an infection. If you have ever had a sore that turned into an infection, then you know exactly what I am talking about because this exactly the same way unforgiveness works. Whatever was done to you pierced your skin, but if you keep prying it open and looking at the wound, it will not be able to heal... instead, because it is continually exposed to the dirty air, it becomes infected. That infection in the spiritual realm is welcoming to unclean spirits, which fester the wound even more. If something is not done, the person ends up facing demonic harassment and torture and becomes a very bitter and unhappy person. I have personally witnessed people living a bitter, miserable, and unhappy life. It is not pretty.

Consider this a solid literal warning that a person can fall into the hands of demonic spirits for torment and harassment if they are unforgiving and bitter inside. I have seen it repeatedly; it is not an uncommon scene to find a person harassed by demons because of bitterness. Remember, unforgiveness is a deadly poison that separates you from God's forgiveness, but it also gives you over to tormenting spirits. And bitterness is also known in the Bible as spiritual poison:

Acts 8:23, *"For I perceive that thou art in the gall (poison) of bitterness, and in the bond of iniquity."*

Unforgiveness will put you into the hands of **tormenting spirits**. This is the last thing you need when you are seeking healing for your soul! Unforgiveness not only gives demons the right or ability to torment you, but it also prevents God from forgiving your sins! It puts up a wall in your relationship with your heavenly Father.

Matthew 18:32-35 reads, *"Then his lord, after that he had called him, said unto him, O thou wicked servant, I forgave thee all that debt, because thou desiredst me: Shouldest not thou also have had compassion on thy fellow servant, even as I had pity on thee? And his lord was wroth,(angry) and delivered him to the tormentors, till he should pay all that was due unto him. So likewise, shall my heavenly Father do also unto you, if ye from your hearts forgive not everyone his brother their trespasses."*

Beyond this, bitterness is also a common means for a born-again believer to become spiritually defiled, that is, polluted or unclean spiritually. Notice the word '*many*' in the verse below. This is a standard means for people to become defiled and open themselves up for spiritual harassment from the enemy.

Hebrews 12:15 says, *"Looking diligently lest any man fail of the grace of God; lest any root of bitterness springing up trouble you, and thereby many be defiled."*

Reasons You Need to Get Rid of Unforgiveness and Forgive

1. Unforgiveness carries a root of bitterness, which will spring up, defile, and contaminate your relationships with your spouse, children, friends, and all others you come in contact with, including God. When we forgive and remain free from bitterness, the door for Satan to bring a multitude of disasters into our lives is closed! Remember the scripture on the law of sowing and reaping:

Galatians 6:7 says, *"Do not be deceived; God is not mocked, for you reap whatever you sow"*

2. God will forgive you of your sins only when you forgive others. Jesus said:

Luke 6:37, *Judge not, and ye shall not be judged; condemn not, and ye shall not be condemned; forgive, and ye shall be forgiven.*

3. Unforgiving people are hurting people, and they hurt others. Forgive profoundly and allow the Holy Spirit to heal your hurting heart; this act will free you from hurting others.

4. Unforgiveness weakens your prayer power, particularly when we're praying for people. It even weakens our salvation prayers for others, including our family and loved ones resulting in them going unsaved for years. The Bible shows we that must forgive when we stand praying:

For verily I say unto you, That whosoever shall say unto this mountain, Be thou removed, and be thou cast into the sea; and shall not doubt in his heart but shall believe that those things which he saith shall come to pass; he shall have whatsoever he saith. Therefore, I say unto you, what things soever ye desire, when ye pray, believe that ye receive them, and ye shall have them. And when ye stand praying, FORGIVE, IF YE HAVE OUGHT AGAINST ANY: THAT YOUR FATHER ALSO WHICH IS IN HEAVEN MAY FORGIVE YOU YOUR TRESPASSES. ... BUT IF YE DO NOT FORGIVE, NEITHER WILL YOUR FATHER WHICH IS IN HEAVEN FORGIVE YOUR TRESPASSES. Mark 11:23-26

5. Unforgiveness can cause you to become sick. It can also prevent you from being healed and from maintaining your healing.

6. Unforgiveness can cause or contribute to emotional (or mental) sickness.

7. Unforgiveness can cause financial curses.

8. When you fail to forgive, you will become like the person you criticize, judge, or hold bitterness toward.

9. If men fail to honor their wives (which includes forgiveness), their prayers will be hindered:

1 Peter 3:7, *Likewise, ye husbands, dwell with them according to knowledge, giving honor unto the wife, as unto the weaker vessel, and as being heirs together of the grace of life; that your prayers be not hindered.*

10. Forgiveness of the one who has hurt you is an essential key to your being released from *negative soul ties* (bondage) with them. It is also a key to breaking *generational curses*, particularly the *deep forgiveness of a mother or father.*

11. You will never rise to greatness in God, ministry, and relationships until you forgive those who have hurt you from your heart. This is particularly true in your marriage. Hurt, bitterness, and rejection (even the ones you've forgotten or thought were buried!) toward your parents can cause distrust in your marriage, even comparing your parents' negative qualities to your spouse. Forgiveness sets you free to adhere to your mate so you can honestly know, trust, and love them more deeply.

This is why Jesus said in Matthew 19:5, *For this cause shall a man leave father and mother and shall cleave to his wife: and they twain shall be one flesh.*

What Are the Signs of Unforgiveness in Your Life?

1. You still feel hurt or rejected by what they did. You think about it all the time, and you are triggered.

2. You are deeply disappointed in someone, yourself, life, or God.

3. You would like to get even with a person and hurt them back. You have a "grudge."

4. *The presence of cancer, arthritis, self-pity, self-condemnation, criticism, depression, or negativity in our lives is almost always rooted in unforgiveness.*

5. The presence of many illnesses in your life. There is almost always significant unforgiveness when one has cancer, arthritis, or other auto-immune conditions.

KNOW THIS: UNFORGIVENESS IS SIN- PLAIN AND SIMPLE

What Do You Lose from Unforgiveness?

1. It opens the door for Satan to attack you in your finances

2. It can cause physical, emotional, or mental sickness

3. It can attack your marriage partner and/or our children (See Matthew 18:21-25).

4. In negative ways, you become like the person you judge!

5. An unforgiving heart robs you of peace, joy, and health.

6. You lose much of the Presence of God.

7. Your Heavenly Father will not forgive you of your sins (Mark 11:25)

Extending Forgiveness

The reason you desperately want to forgive is so the healing power of Holy Spirit won't be hindered or blocked by unforgiveness. You don't want to be bound and separated from God's awesome, forgiving, and healing power for your life. It is vital to extend forgiveness and release your feelings against others so that the Holy Spirit's mighty healing and forgiving power can heal and restore your soul. You simply can't receive healing for yourself when you're in a position of unforgiveness.

Mark 11:25-26 states, *"And when ye stand praying, forgive, if ye have aught against any: that your Father also which is in heaven may forgive you your trespasses. But if ye do not forgive, neither will your Father which is in heaven forgive your trespasses."*

Inner healing requires God's forgiveness. When you don't extend forgiveness, you're in spiritual darkness and separation from God.

1 John 2:11, "But he that hateth his brother is in darkness, and walketh in darkness, and knoweth not whither he goeth, because that darkness hath blinded his eyes."

To receive complete healing for your soul, it is essential to release feelings of bitterness and extend forgiveness to others. Forgiving others will welcome the healing power of the Holy Spirit into your life where you're no longer hindered or bound.

Realize Who You Are in Christ

Realizing your identity in Christ is vital to your healing process. When you know that you are a new creation in Christ, freed from the darkness of your past, forgiven of your sins, and freedom and healing are yours because of the Blood that Christ shed for you, you will stop feeding on the lies of insecurity, guilt, and pain from the devil.

There is an allegory about two men on our shoulders, and whichever one you listen to will crowd the other one out. This is absolutely true concerning how you handle God's voice and the devil's voice. "You need to be discerning of the voice of the devil… it is your responsibility not to give consideration (or pay attention) to it!"

It is absolutely vital that you do NOT listen or pay attention to the voice of the devil in your mind. God's Word tells us that we need to take every thought captive to the obedience to Christ:

> **2 Corinthians 10:4 reads,** *"Casting down imaginations, and every high thing that exalteth itself against the knowledge of God and bringing into captivity every thought to the obedience of Christ."*

One thing we need to watch out for is condemnation and fear. Both of these come from the enemy. "*What if*" thinking is always a giveaway that the devil is doing the speaking, not you. You need to realize you're a new creation in Christ; therefore, walk it out and do not pay him any mind! The demons are nothing to mess with; they are powerful spiritual beings, and without Christ, they are not yet disarmed in your life (see Colossians 2:13-15).

When you listen to more of what God says and not the devil, you open the door for a closer relationship with God. If you reach out to God and seek a deeper relationship with Him, He will draw near to you, you will find him, and have more intimacy with Him. God's Word is clear about this fact:

> **Luke 11:9-10 reads,** *"And I say unto you, Ask, and it shall be given you; seek, and ye shall find; knock, and it shall be opened unto you. For every one that asketh receiveth; and he that seeketh findeth; and to him that knocketh it shall be opened."*

> Also, **James 4:8 says**, *"Draw nigh to God, and he will draw nigh to you..."*

The relationship is yours for the taking! Christ wanted this relationship with you so badly that He gave *His life* for it! He paid a great price for you! Your heavenly Father wants this intimate relationship with you even more than you do. The kind of relationship God wants is an intimate love relationship...**A LOVE BOND Relationship.**

If you are not a Christian and would like to accept Jesus right now as your Lord and Savior, let's go before Him now with a prayer like this:

"Lord Jesus Christ, I realize I am a sinner. I believe you died and shed your blood for the remission of my sins so that I may have eternal life. Right now, I turn from my sins and ask that you come into my life, changing me into a new person and washing all my sins away.
I receive you as my personal Lord and Savior. Amen."

Forgive Yourself

Forgiving yourself is a vital step in seeking inner healing. You need to love and appreciate the person Christ has made you! We must see "us" for who we are in Christ. If you continue to beat yourself up for your past failures after the Blood of Christ has washed them away, then you are, in reality, denying the very work of the cross.

Forgive yourself by going to that pain and emotional wound that is hidden deep within you and confront it with the Word and the healing love of Christ. Here are a few (of many) good verses to meditate on:

Psalms 103:12, "As far as the east is from the west, so far hath he removed our transgressions from us."

Romans 5:1, "Therefore being justified by faith, we have peace with God through our Lord Jesus Christ."

Isaiah 43:25, "I, even I, am he that blotteth out thy transgressions for mine own sake and will not remember thy sins."

Hebrews 10:22 says, "…draw near with a true heart in full assurance of faith, having our hearts sprinkled from an evil conscience, and our bodies washed with pure water."

Colossians 1:22-23, "…he has brought you back as his friends. He has done this through his death on the cross in his own human body. As a result, he has brought you into the very presence of God, and you are holy and blameless as you stand before him without a single fault. But you must continue to believe this truth and stand in it firmly. Do not drift away from the assurance you received when you heard the Good News. The Good News has been preached all over the world, and I, Paul, have been appointed by God to proclaim it." (NLT)

Knowing that Jesus has paid for your emotional wounds, hurts, pains, and sorrows, tell the roots of all inner hurt, painful memories, and emotional affliction to leave in the name of Jesus. Then, call upon Jesus to remove those things from you.

You might pray something like this:

"Lord Jesus, I love you. Thank you for bearing my burden on the cross. I ask that you take the roots of all my inner hurts, painful memories, and emotional wounds of _____ from me right now.

I submit them to you and accept your peace in place of those things which I am giving up."

How Do We Forgive Others?

Remember, extending forgiveness does not let them off God's hook, you are merely releasing *your* soul from the bondage that unforgiveness brought you under. You are not forgiving them for their benefit but for your own good! Your soul, not theirs, is what is held in bondage because of the feelings you have allowed to harbor inside you. Why should you allow what they have done to continue to bring you under bondage? I would not! I would get that poison out of my heart. This is why you must give it to the Lord and seek Him to heal the wounds they have caused.

Forgiving others can be extremely hard, but it is essential if you want to break out of the bondage that it has brought you under. Forgiving others opens you up for the Lord to begin healing your soul (inner healing). Unforgiveness blocks you from receiving God's forgiveness of your sins, it puts up a wall between you and the source of your healing.

Matthew 6:15, *"But if ye forgive not men their trespasses, neither will your Father forgive your trespasses."*

Forgiveness is a choice. You must choose to forgive those who have done you wrong, then lay the whole mess in God's hands and leave it there. Give your hurts and hard feelings to Him. You may be thinking: "That person has NO clue what they have done to me! They do not deserve anything at all, much less *MY forgiveness*!" We understand and hear you loud and clear. They certainly do not deserve your forgiveness, much less God's...but none of us deserve what Jesus did for us either. We all have sinned. A-L-L. Think about Jesus and how they murdered Him. Neither you nor I were beaten, tortured, and crucified, yet one of the last words that left His mouth before his death were the cries: "*Father, forgive them, for they do not know what they do."* Look at the deep, rich mercy and love that Jesus has towards us... none of us deserve it! But He loves us for who we are, not because of what we have done. He wanted a relationship with you so much that He gave His life for it!

My heart breaks, and tears flow every time I think about this. If we were on the cross and our sides were pierced with swords, a crown of thorns had been shoved on our heads, and our feet and hands had spikes driven through them, could we honestly look to the Father and ask to forgive them? I can tell you right now that the answer would be a big fat NO, but look at the depth of God's love for us! God's deep love for us was expressed through Jesus' death on the cross. Walking in forgiveness, practicing forgiveness as a way of life, and praying blessings on those who hurt you are keys to good physical, emotional, and mental health.

Jesus was clear that if we are to be forgiven, *we must forgive others*. When you grasp what Jesus has done for you, it makes it a lot easier to pass that grace along to others. Once you begin to comprehend the great expression of love that was towards you, that same love will begin to grow in your heart and flow out to others. It is important to grow in God's love and become well aware of how deep and rich it is. When you understand His love for you, you will find that forgiving others comes naturally, and the choice becomes much easier to make.

Here are some steps to help you get closer to forgiving others:

1. Recognize and repent of the sin of judging, of unforgiveness, of having a wrong attitude toward the person who has hurt you. Remember that you and I hurt others also, and we often need forgiveness.

2. Asking for God's help to decide to forgive.

3. Get alone with God and intercede for the person who has hurt you. Intercession is powerful in producing forgiveness.

4. Seek emotional healing of the hurts causing the unforgiveness. Allow the pain to leave you by praying in tongues! Even anger can depart with intense praying in tongues!

5. Revoke the legal right for bitterness and unforgiveness to remain. Choose to forgive.

6. Ask God to regain the surrendered ground that gave bitterness a "foothold" or opportunity to take root.

This statement was said earlier, and it bears repeating: *When you do not want to believe the truth, you protect your unforgiveness and emotional pain and live in a false reality!* The way you get healing is to FACE the truth and bring it to JESUS because He already knows what is there. When you challenge what gives you security (unforgiveness and bitterness), you feel threatened, and anger arises, giving the tormenting spirits the right to come into the situation. And you wonder why you are in the shape you are in.

In the first two chapters of Job, Satan brings destruction to his sons and daughters, to his wealth, and brings boils to his body. In Job 5:22, God does not tell Job to pray and fast or to seek prayer from others but commands Job to laugh at this incredible trial in his life, "At destruction and famine *thou shall laugh.*" God refers to a *holy laugh* of faith, submissiveness, and *warfare.* It is powerful. Please try and do it with persistence because I know it will work.

7. Sometimes, you must forgive others in person, over the telephone, or by letter. However, sometimes, it is impossible to go to that person, or it's best not to. They might even be dead. In that case, you must express your forgiveness for them directly to God.

8. Continually thank God for everything He and others have given and done for you. This will help you forgive everyone and overcome self-pity, mumbling, and complaining (which are twins of unforgiveness!).

Many have been deeply rejected or hurt by others. Jesus calls you to forgive as He has forgiven you. Such deep forgiveness can often only come through healing from the rejection and hurts of others.

Unforgiveness + God's Love = Forgiveness

Unforgiveness is taking something that belongs to God and taking matters into your own hands. God's Word tells you clearly that you should allow God to bring His wrath upon that person and let Him have the room to repay those who wrong us:

> **Romans 12:19**, *"Dearly beloved, avenge not yourselves, but rather give place unto wrath: for it is written, Vengeance is mine; I will repay, saith the Lord."*

Those who have wronged you will reap what they sow! No doubt about it. If you choose to forgive somebody, they may be off your hook, but that does not mean they are off God's. God's Word tells us clearly that what we sow, we shall reap:

> **Galatians 6:7**, *"Be not deceived; God is not mocked: for whatsoever a man soweth, that shall he also reap."*

Unforgiveness is a form of hatred, which is a lack of love. If you are bitter with somebody, then the love of Christ is not flowing through you. So, how do we solve that problem? We need to grow in God's love. We need to realize the deep and beautiful love He has for us. When we walk in unforgiveness, we're taking something that belongs to God and taking matters into your own hands, but God loves you too much for you to do that. God's Word tells you clearly that you should allow God to bring His wrath upon that person and let Him have the room to repay those who wronged you. God does not want you to carry this vengeance in your heart. Because God loves you, He will handle it and ensure justice is served. As you learn of His love for you, your spirit will respond, and you will love Him in return.

Romans 12:19, *"Dearly beloved, avenge not yourselves, but rather give place unto wrath: for it is written, Vengeance is mine; I will repay, saith the Lord."*

Those who have wronged you will reap what they sow! No doubt about it. When you choose to forgive somebody, they may be off your hook, but that does not mean they are off God's. God's Word tells us clearly that what we sow, we shall reap:

Galatians 6:7, *"Be not deceived; God is not mocked: for whatsoever a man soweth, that shall he also reap."*

When you release unforgiveness and open your hearts to forgiveness, now the love of God begins to flow through you. How does one come to know the love of God? By spending time with Him. Studying God's Word will help you see what the Bible says about His great love for you. The more you develop an intimate relationship with God, you will come to know His love.

Here are some verses to help you get started:

John 10:11, 15:13, *"I am the good shepherd: the good shepherd giveth his life for the sheep... Greater love hath no man than this, that a man lay down his life for his friends."*

1 Corinthians 2:9, *"But as it is written, Eye hath not seen, nor ear heard, neither have entered into the heart of man, the things which God hath prepared for them that love him."*

Romans 2:4, *"Or despises thou the riches of his goodness and forbearance and longsuffering; not knowing that the goodness of God leadeth thee to repentance?"*

1 John 3:1, *"Behold, what manner of love the Father hath bestowed upon us, that we should be called the sons of God..."*

Look at this one... you are not loved for what you have done but because of who you are! Even before you came to Christ, He loved you so much that He died for you!

Romans 5:8, *"But God showed his great love for us by sending Christ to die for us while we were still sinners." (NLT)*

1 John 4:9, *"In this was manifested the love of God toward us, because that God sent His only begotten Son into the world, that we might live through him."*

If you have a tough time forgiving others, it is because the love of Jesus is not flowing through you. How do you solve this problem? Start working on your relationship, that LOVE BOND with your heavenly Father so you can come to know of His great love for you, and then your spirit will respond, and His love will begin to flow through you naturally. When that starts to happen, forgiving those who have wronged you will become much more easier.

It is nearly impossible for somebody who is flowing in God's love to hold bitterness (a form of hate) inside! If you struggle with bitterness, it is because you lack Jesus's love in your life! You need to become grounded and rooted in Christ's love if you want His love to flow through you! Jesus made it very clear that if you love Him, keeping His commandments will naturally follow. If you love Jesus, carrying out His love will come naturally to you:

John 14:23, *"Jesus answered and said unto him, If a man lovs me, he will keep my words: and my Father will love him, and we will come unto him, and make our abode with him."*

What was His significant commandment? To let His love flow through you to others around you, and love them as He has loved us:

John 13:34, *"A new commandment I give unto you, that ye love one another; as I have loved you, that ye also love one another."*

Set It on the Back Burner

First, put everything that bothers you on the back burner and seek your heavenly Father's love. Seek a living relationship with Him and learn of His deep love for you—it will change your life!

Second, choose to release those hurt feelings and allow God to heal the wounds. As you grow in His love, this choice will become much easier to walk out. When you continue seeking a loving relationship with Him, it will change your whole perspective on life, and forgiving others will come naturally. Healing of those wounds will also become a genuine and tangible reality.

Here is a prayer to help you extend forgiveness to others, God, or even yourself.

Prayer Of Forgiveness

In Jesus Name I choose to forgive_____

I break the power of their words over me,

I break the victim spirit off of me,

I rebuke the fear of man that I have lived under,

I now cancel my bond with them,

I take back my true identity,

I will not live under this oppression,

I now receive my forever love,

I am now free to live and to love.

I remove all lingering residue, and I ask that courage begins to rise,

I receive my new true identity beginning to emerge, and I have the courage to set proper boundaries

I have the courage to leave when I need to walk out of a situation

I have the freedom, Lord, to live in love with YOU and to live out of that relationship with YOU

IN JESUS NAME. Amen.

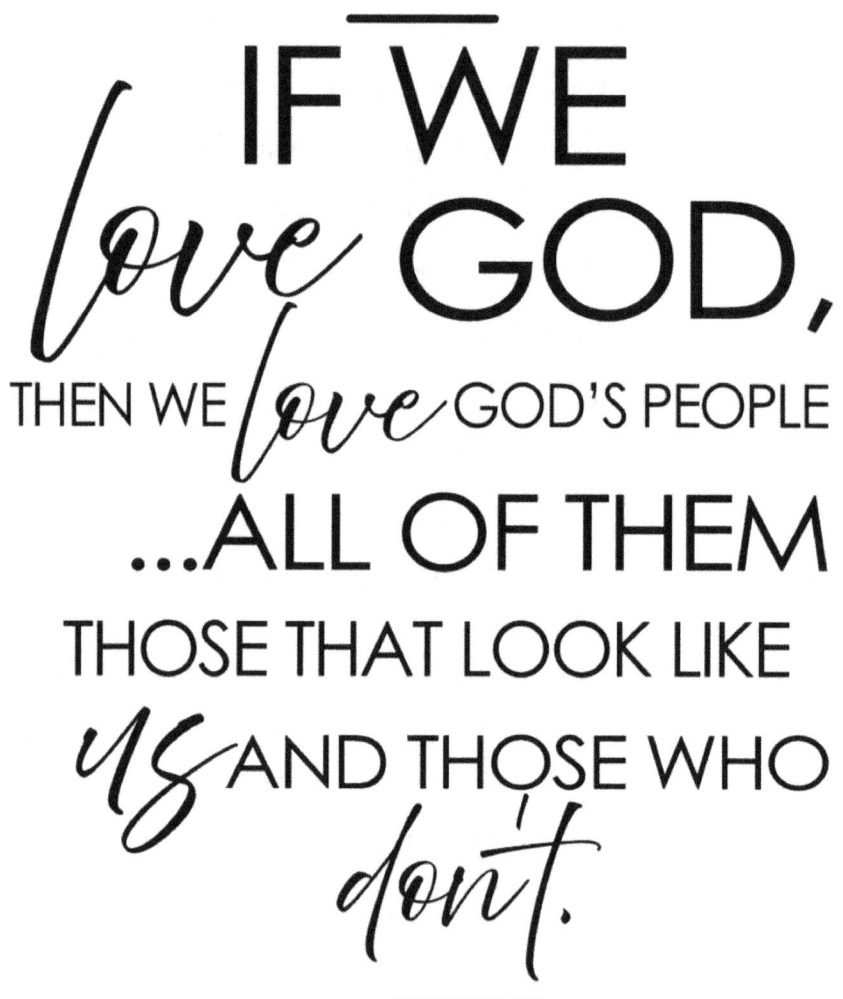

IF WE *love* GOD, THEN WE *love* GOD'S PEOPLE ...ALL OF THEM THOSE THAT LOOK LIKE *us* AND THOSE WHO *don't.*

CHAPTER 7

HEALING RACIAL WOUNDS JESUS' WAY

At the back of this chapter, you will find a questionnaire and definitions of these terms, specifically inserted to provide knowledge, awareness, and understanding of the racial wounds of yesterday, which are still reinforcing the racial traumas of today.

In 2020, a confident Pastor from Hammond, Indiana, said a wild yet honest and humble prayer asking God to bring the Hispanic community to Anthem Church, a growing parish in the State of Indiana where the white race makes up 84.2% of the population, according to the US Census 2020. Who knew that through a pandemic, God would answer the Pastor's wild and bodacious prayer, bringing a massive increase in the Latino community to his growing church? That increase in cultural representation opened the door for God to heal many racial wounds and bring unity within the Body of Christ. It's incredible what can happen when we stand on God's powerful Word.

1 John 5:14 says, "*This is the confidence we have in approaching God: that if we ask anything according to his will, he hears us.*"

Healing racial wounds and unity with each other is God's will. Still, the talks concerning racism have been disregarded and omitted in conversations everywhere---schools, church, work, and politics. Sharing personal stories of racism and the trauma that stems from it is very heavy and hard for some even to unpack all, but our Lord and Savior Jesus can handle it.

Matthew 11:28-30, *28 Then Jesus said, "Come to me, all of you who are weary and carry heavy burdens, and I will give you rest. 29 Take my yoke upon you. Let me teach you, because I am humble and gentle at heart, and you will find rest for your souls. 30 For my yoke is easy to bear, and the burden I give you is light."*

God's people are burdened with personal experiences of hate or strong dislike toward their own race as well as other races. Believers are filled with images and wounds of *the historical trauma of slavery, discrimination in the workplace and schools,* and the *racial slurs* we've adopted as our very own way of getting revenge and self-gratification that keeps us weary and in bondage from receiving our healing.

1 Corinthians 1:10, *I appeal to you, brothers and sisters, in the name of our Lord Jesus Christ, that all of you agree with one another in what you say and that there be no divisions among you, but that you be perfectly united in mind and thought.*

Psalms 133:1, *How good and pleasant it is when God's people live together in unity!*

When we are healed from racial traumas and wounds of the past, and today, God's people shall live together in unity. The Lord is not concerned about the color of one's skin when it comes to salvation, healing, and freedom. However, God is not at all at peace when injustice is done to His people because of a difference in status, class, or the color of their skin, a skin color God himself created. God's desire for us all is unity in mind and thought. That includes every racist thought, action, and slur---we've said, heard, or believed shall be brought under subjection so that we as Believers and our entire race and bloodline will not be disqualified.

1 Corinthians 9:27, *"But I discipline my body and bring it into subjection, lest, when I have preached to others, I myself should become disqualified."*

As you continue to read, you will receive instructions to discipline you in faith. The first key is acknowledging that Christ died for all, and all are God's children through faith!

Galatians 3:26-28, *26* *"So in Christ Jesus you are all children of God through faith, 27 for all of you who were baptized into Christ have clothed yourselves with Christ. 28 There is neither Jew nor Gentile, neither slave nor free, nor is there male and female, for you are all one in Christ Jesus."*

Adam Clarke (1762-1832) was a Methodist theologian and scholar who wrote the most comprehensive biblical commentaries of his day. He taught that the Bible ultimately interprets God's nature and will. Here's Clarke's Commentary on Jeremiah 13:23:

Jeremiah 13:23 states, *"Can the Ethiopian change the color of his skin Or the leopard take away his spots? Neither can you start doing good, for you have always done evil."*

Clark wrote: "Can a black (person), at his own pleasure, change the color of his skin? Can the leopard at will change the variety of his spots? These things are natural to them, and they cannot be altered; so, sin, and especially your attachment to idolatry, has become second nature, and we may as well expect the Ethiopian to change his skin and the leopard his spots as you to do good, who have been accustomed to do evil. It is a matter of the utmost difficulty to get a sinner, deeply rooted in vicious habits, brought to the knowledge of himself and God. But the expression does not imply that the thing is as impossible in a moral as it is in a natural sense: it only shows that it is extremely difficult and not to be often expected, and a thousand matters of fact prove the truth of this. But still, what is impossible for man is possible for God."

Matthew 19:26 states that *Jesus looked at them and said, "With man this is impossible, but with God all things are possible."*

Even though our God doesn't treat us unjustly because of the color of our skin, we must not be clueless about the current world we live in, where injustices happen every single day because of racism, colorism, and prejudice. Ever since Adam and Eve sinned in the garden, we've lived in a fallen world. We struggle with sin daily, experience heartache and pain, witness natural disasters, and experience trauma that has questioned our faith at times. The struggle is not just for some; this is not a Black or

White thing. No, we all, every last of us, have our own experience of living in a fallen world because we each have fallen; yet Jesus came to save the world.

John 12:47 reads, *"If anyone hears my words and does not keep them, I do not judge him; for I did not come to judge the world but to save the world."*

So, how do you save a fallen world with so much historical trauma that still triggers the racial wounds of today? With inner healing.

- By seeking God's plan and exchanging your racial wounds for God's healing. Read *Isaiah 57:18-19*
- By surrendering the hurt and things you don't understand or never will for God's peace.

Read *Philippians 4:6*

- By asking for compassion. Read *Ephesians 4:32*

Before we can begin to heal the racial wounds of yesterday and today and stand in the gap for the ones in the future, we need to pray, ask God for the spirit of compassion, and welcome it wholeheartedly into our hearts.

You may be thinking you've never put innocent people into a cage, attempted to take down a group of people because of hatred and jealousy, or ever been racist to anyone in your life. However, even if this is true, you have hurt someone with your words, beliefs, and judgments, and it might have been yourself. Or maybe you were jealous at a point in your life, lived a life of comparison, and were mad at God because you weren't content with your situation. Whether the sin was great or small, our God is no respecter of persons. God does not ignore nor change His standards for anyone, the slave master or the one who uses foul language and lies from time to time. God has an unconditional love for everyone He created, and that's where Jesus comes in. He came and died for ALL, not some, because WE ALL have sinned and do need the glory of God.

Romans 3:23-27, 23 *"for all have sinned and fall short of the glory of God, **24** and are justified by his grace as a gift, through the redemption that is* *in Christ Jesus, 25 whom God put forward as a propitiation by his blood, to be received by faith. This was to show God's righteousness, because in his divine forbearance he had passed over former sins. 26 It was to show his righteousness at the present time, so that he might be just and the justifier of the one who has faith in Jesus. 27 Then what becomes of our boasting? It is excluded. By what kind of law? By a law of works? No, but by the law of faith."*

We urgently need God's faith and Christ-centered healing for the Lord to meet us, heal us, and help us love our neighbor and ourselves.

Where does the Lord meet us?

The Lord meets us right where we're at. But do we know that? Do we really believe that God is meeting us right where we are?

The scripture Psalm 34: 4-7 NIV reads, *4 "I sought the Lord, and he answered me; He delivered me from all my fears. 5 Those who look to him are radiant; their faces are never covered with shame. 6 This poor man called, and the Lord heard him; He saved him out of all his troubles. 7 The angel of the Lord encamps around those who fear him, and he delivers them."*

+ If we're in pain, Jesus provides healing.
+ If we're confused or don't understand, the Holy Spirit will provide the answers.
+ If we're burdened with past and present trauma, Jesus provides rest.
+ If we need saving, the Lord delivers us.

Before we dive deeper into this chapter, take a moment to pray. Dear Lord, reveal any racial wounds I have knowingly or unknowingly, even the ones that are suppressed. Show me the racial wounds of other races so I can understand. Lord, I ask that you give me the spirit of compassion. In Jesus Name, Amen.

Let's Begin.

What is Racial Trauma? What are Racial Wounds?

According to Mental Health America, racial trauma is the mental and emotional injury caused by encounters with racial bias and ethnic discrimination, racism, and hate crimes.

Racism is prejudice or antagonism directed only against minority people/persons and marginalized racial and ethnic groups.

Racial wounds are the products and aftermath of racism and racial trauma experienced, such as PTSD, anxiety, avoidance behavior, substance abuse, depression, disassociation, weathering, negative thoughts, and increased sensitivity and reactivity.

Some may say racism is non-existent because our country has come a long way from slavery, redlining, and Jim Crow Laws; however, that is far from true. Other forms of racism are called systematic racism, and that is still blatantly present in housing, work, marriages, churches, music, entertainment, wealth distribution, politics, media, health care access, and education. Systematic racism is not always conscious, explicit, or readily evident for one to recognize and understand.

- It can come in the form of laws like Title 42, where Latino children were seen locked in cages near the South Border.
- Or it can be a lack of media attention, like when 300,000 girls who went missing in 2020 were Black, and there was little or no media attention at all provided.
- Or the 339% increase in Asian hate crimes because of COVID-19 being called the "China Virus."
- Or gerrymandering, the deliberate redrawing of electoral district boundaries to favor the political party in power. Gerrymandering makes some people's votes count less than others, depriving them of full representation.

These aren't yesterday's traumas of the past; these are currently happening right now, proving that racism still exists today.

These are all examples below of how racial trauma affects everyday people historically and generationally:

Distress relating to the trauma: This may cause a person to think about and relive an event continually. Some people have flashbacks or nightmares.

Avoiding things that remind the person of the trauma: This can negatively affect a person's life in many ways. For example, a person who experiences racism at college may leave school, while a person who experiences racism in a police interaction may fear the police or run when they see them. The person experiences intense anxiety or depression relating to the trauma. Trauma can affect someone at any time or continuously—negative thoughts about self, other people, or the world. For example, a person might lose trust in others or worry that all authority figures want to harm them.

Increased sensitivity and reactivity: A person may startle easily and become more hypervigilant to their surroundings. This mindset may increase exposure to further trauma, such as when a person is afraid of the police and behaves anxiously when the police are around.

Research shows that when a person of color experiences a racist threat, the brain is wired to prepare the body to fight or flight. Because of repeated racist incidents, the traumatic stress is compounded and not adequately dealt with, so the brain and body don't fully stand down. The person remains racially traumatized, which triggers a physical and emotional response, which in turn feeds the racial trauma. So, they get stuck in an endless loop.

Historical racism may have weakened many people's DNA, causing racial trauma to be passed down to future generations. The church prays, cultures pray, and we all pray, yet there are still battles with the psychological symptoms of racial trauma.

Inner Healing and Deliverance from Racial Trauma

We, as the body of Christ, must acknowledge that racial trauma exists. Many Christians do not recognize or even know nor understand they are in racial trauma bondage, nor do they recognize their racial wounds, strongholds, or the open "gates" or "doors" that allow darkness to influence them.

The scripture warns us of this in Hosea and Isaiah, and it's still applicable today:

> *"My people are destroyed for lack of knowledge." - Hosea 4:6*

What prevents many people from knowing the racial trauma and wounds that hindered us in our faith is denial that some are privileged and wreaking the undue benefit of it without helping others to have the same advantage and playing field.

What is Privilege?

Privilege is where one group of people receives "an invisible package of unearned assets." In Western countries, many like to call it "White Privilege," where one who is born white is assumed to have certain privileges regardless of any personal skills or accomplishments. But in actuality, privilege dates back to Jesus' day. God chose the Jews for special blessings; they had a covenant relationship with God; consequently, they looked down on the Gentiles. The Jews considered themselves superior to Gentiles, an attitude that drove a deep-seated wedge of hostility between the two groups. But Jesus Christ settled the long-standing division and obliterated the distinction between Jew and Gentile. God saw that both Jews and the Gentiles were sinners and ALL needed saving through grace; yet through Jesus Christ's burial and resurrection, we ALL are justified through faith.

Romans 3:23-24 23 *"For everyone has sinned; we all fall short of God's glorious standard. **24** Yet God, in his grace, freely makes us right in his sight. He did this through Christ Jesus when he freed us from the penalty for our sins."*

Galatians 3:26-29 26 *"For you are all children of God through faith in Christ Jesus. 27 And all who have been united with Christ in baptism have put on Christ, like putting on new clothes. 28 There is no longer Jew or Gentile, slave or free, male and female. For you are all one in Christ Jesus. 29 And now that you belong to Christ, you are the true children[d] of Abraham. You are his heirs, and God's promise to Abraham belongs to you."*

Through the scriptures, you can see that God chooses particular people, but not for selfish gain. God's purpose for choosing any nation, person, or people is so that others would be blessed through them. The children of Israel, Jesus Christ, and the Jewish people were all chosen by God so nations can be blessed through them.

In **Genesis 12:2-3, 2,** *"I will make you into a great nation. I will bless you and make you famous, and you will be a blessing to others. 3 I will bless those who bless you and curse those who treat you with contempt. All the families on earth will be blessed through you."*

Pay close attention to that last line, "All the families on earth will be blessed through you." Since Jesus has torn the veil since the days of Abraham and the Old Testament, we ALL have access to God. God was done with the holy of the Holy Temple and through with the religious system. We, too, should be done with the systems of this world that do not line up with God's plan through Jesus Christ because we ALL are privileged, White, Black, male, and female, and are called to use our privilege to bless others and be a blessing to others. As believers of Christ, we no longer should remain blind to the racial traumas and poor conditions of God's people… ALL God's people.

So, is privilege real? It is. Because of a fallen world, some have rights in this world more than others; however, there is no such thing in God's eyes that a race is superior to another. Is it fair? No. But scripture tells us that greater is He that is in me than He that is in the world.

1 John 4:4 reads, *"You, dear children, are from God and have overcome them because the one who is in you is greater than the one who is in the world."*

Therefore, we may be **IN** this world, but we are not **OF** it. As Believers and God's people with more privilege than anyone, we do not conform to this world, but we are transformed by the renewing of our minds. Jesus points out that the ultimate thing for the privileged to do for others is to get in the fight and help bring forth change!

In the scripture in **Luke 11:46,** *Jesus replied, "And you experts in the law, woe to you, because you load people down with burdens they can hardly carry, and you your-selves will not lift one finger to help them."*

Isaiah 5:13 reads, *"So, my people will go into exile far away because they do not know me. Those who are great and honored will starve, and the common people will die of thirst."*

When Believers and Leaders are blind to the racial trauma, it affects us all: the honorable, the great, the privileged, basically an entire multitude of people. When we become blind to the demonic attacks of past and current racial trauma and the wounds, we're dismissing the present-day emotional, spiritual, and physical problems stemming from traumatic events and grievous sins from earlier generations, which many individuals are now reaping a harvest of depression, anxiety, and fear, as well as various physical problems. Racial wounds hinder Christians in this current generation in their spiritual walk from hearing or seeing God, nor are they able to get free from the struggles of life.

When we surrender the racial traumas and wounds of yesterday and the present day, Jesus takes our wounds and, in exchange, gives us freedom from our wounds. One of Christ's purposes in coming to earth was to destroy the works of the devil.

1 John 3:8-10, *"But when people keep on sinning, it shows that they belong to the devil, who has been sinning since the beginning. But the Son of God came to destroy the works of the devil. 9 Those who have been born into God's family do not make a practice of sinning, because God's life[a] is in them. So, they can't keep on sinning because they are children of God. 10 So now we can tell who are children of God and who are children of the devil. Anyone who does not live righteously and does not love other believers[b] does not belong to God."*

The scripture doesn't say White, Black, or Brown believers. It says *"other Believers."* When we live righteously and belong to God, we love other believers regardless of color, ethnicity, or cultural/environmental background.   Believers should always reference Jesus' greatest commandment whenever they doubt how to love others.

Matthew 22:37-39, *Jesus replied: "'Love the Lord your God with all your heart and with all your soul and with all your mind.' This is the first and greatest commandment. And the second is like it: 'Love your neighbor as yourself.'"*

Jesus taught us the importance of loving ourselves in Christ, which is critical in loving others; many do not even like ourselves. Have you ever heard the phrase, "Hurt People Hurt People"? Colorism is an example of this; being lighter meant more privilege and being regarded as more beautiful than the darker skinned. Slave owners used skin color to create division within the Black and Brown races, which still to this day affects races within their communities and families and even self-hatred amongst themselves and others. This seed of self-hatred and self-rejection was not at all God's idea. In the Bible, The Song of Solomon highlights the romantic love King Solomon had for the young Shulamite woman,

1 Song of Solomon 1:5, *I am dark but beautiful, O women of Jerusalem— dark as the tents of Kedar, dark as the curtains of Solomon's tents.*

The very skin tone he highlights in this verse is the skin tone that's experienced so much hatred amongst God's people. More so, God did not curse his people by giving them "Black skin." God did not curse Ham; Noah cursed Ham's son Canaan. In Genesis 9, it was not because Ham was Black or dark-skinned but because Ham was disobedient and brought shame to his father, Noah. On the flip side, Ham had four children, and Canaan was the only one cursed. Satan has twisted the scripture into a lie. Note, I said Satan and not slave owners, even though pro-slavery preachers used this twisted lie from Satan to justify the hellish behaviors toward dark-skinned people. The Bible says that Satan is the only one who twists scripture, just like he twisted scripture against Jesus when our Lord was led up by the spirit to be tempted. Read Matthew 4:1-11. The devil is the only one behind twisting God's Word to create division and sow seeds of discord among God's people. Not the politicians, not your family members, the educational system, or your boss; the real enemy, thief, and liar is Satan.

John 10:10, *The thief comes only to steal, kill, and destroy; I have come that they may have life and have it to the full.*

Today, Satan is still lying and twisting God's truth. There has been great debate on the leading cause of Black deaths in this country, especially Black-on-Black crimes. The argument is that Black and Brown people kill their selves. Although this may be a fact, it isn't the truth. From the Bible days until today, people have killed their people. Jesus himself, being a Jew, was crucified by the Pharisees and the Sadducees, which are the Jews. Whenever there's oppression (prolonged cruelty and unjust cruelty) and hatred toward a people, those are the works of the devil and not of Jesus.

But God...Jesus came to set the captives free and those who were oppressed.

Luke 4:18, *"The Spirit of the Lord is upon Me (the Messiah), Because He has anointed Me to preach the good news to the poor. He has sent Me to announce release (pardon, forgiveness) to the captives, And recovery of sight to the blind, To set free those who are oppressed (downtrodden, bruised, crushed by tragedy)."*

Whenever there is racial trauma, the racial wounds need inner healing Christ's way, not the world's way. There are certain things the world may never understand, but as Believers, we're called to share the good news of Jesus with others and make it known because Jesus Christ lives in us. The good news of Jesus Christ is found in scripture. It's in His Word. You'll get a lot of scripture with this lesson because for true inner healing to occur, we need to stand on God's truth, not tradition, not what's culturally accepted, but God's Word is alive and powerful, dividing what's right and wrong.

Hebrews 4:12, *"For the Word of God is alive and powerful. It is sharper than the sharpest two-edged sword, cutting between soul and spirit, between joint and marrow. It exposes our innermost thoughts and desires."*

Healing requires us to expose the hurt and trauma behind the racial wounds, even the hidden ones we secretly hold on to because the bitterness is comforting to our trauma bonds/bondage. Bitterness and roots from racial trauma can look like: crippling anxiety, fear, aggression, depression, shame, racial slurs, hypervigilance, pessimism, nightmares, substance abuse, flashbacks, and relational dysfunction.

Pulling Up the Roots of Racial Trauma and Wounds in our Heart

In **Matthew 15:13**, *Jesus replied, "Every plant that my heavenly Father has not planted will be pulled up by the roots."*

We must understand people are like sheep, not knowing nor understanding the depth of their actions, words, and thoughts. We need to be taught, and Jesus is the ultimate teacher who guides us to inner healing.

Mark 6:34, *"And Jesus, when He came out, saw a great multitude and was moved with compassion for them, because they were like sheep not having a shepherd. So, He began to teach them many things."*

Hebrews 2:17-18, *"Therefore, in all things He had to be made like His brethren, that He might be a merciful and faithful High Priest in things pertaining to God, to make propitiation for the sins of the people. For in that He Himself has suffered, being tempted, He is able to aid those who are tempted."*

Even though Jesus became sin, he never sinned. He was pure. It's sometimes difficult to pray and trust God's plan for healing without a pure heart. A pure heart doesn't mean being flawless; instead, it means a heart that desires nothing more than to be with God because that truly is all a Believer's life should be about! It's about seeing ourselves as we are, coming to God poor in spirit. We mourn over our very own condition and like the psalmist, we pray Psalm 51:10. Right now, take a moment and pray the scripture, *"Lord, create in me a clean heart, O God, and renew a steadfast spirit within me. Erase any wickedness from my heart and replace it with your love joy, and peace. In Jesus Name, Amen."*

Jesus promises those who embody this pure heart will see God. Only those with a pure heart will know Jesus because that is what Jesus sees.

The Bible says in **Luke 6:45**, *"The good man brings good things out of the good stored up in his heart. For out of the overflow of his heart his mouth speaks."*

Through compassion, forgiveness, peace, and applying God's Word, we can heal from the racial trauma and no longer be bound by the racial wounds of yesterday, today, and even tomorrow.

→ *Compassion helps release all bitterness and roots of racial trauma.*

What does it mean to have compassion? It means you empathize with those suffering, and there's a strong need to feel compelled to help reduce their suffering. It's not always easy to show compassion, especially when we think or believe the person(s) deserve their misfortune or punishment. The Spirit of Compassion and Mercy is a gift from God. If you lack compassion, ask the Holy Spirit to enable you with this gift and attribute of God.

Exodus 34:6-7, 6 *The Lord passed in front of Moses, calling out, "Yahweh! The Lord! The God of compassion and mercy! I am slow to anger and filled with unfailing love and faithfulness. 7 I lavish unfailing love to a thousand generations. I forgive iniquity, rebellion, and sin. But I do not excuse the guilty. I lay the sins of the parents upon their children and grandchildren; the entire family is affected— even children in the third and fourth generations."*

2 Corinthians 1:3-4, 3 *"Praise be to the God and Father of our Lord Jesus Christ, the Father of compassion and the God of all comfort, 4 who comforts us in all our troubles, so that we can comfort those in any trouble with the comfort we ourselves receive from God."*

The people of God desperately need the spirit of compassion like never before in today's world. Our Father is comforting and compassionate and requires us to be the same for others.

→*There's that "F" word again...Forgiveness.*

Before we can heal from what other races have done to us, or even our race, we need to *forgive*. Sometimes, it's hard to forgive people for this kind of racial trauma of slavery, everyday hatred, and systematic racism we witness daily, but we must. If we need to increase our level of forgiveness, we must enhance our humility.

2 Chronicles 7:14, *14 "If my people, which are called by my name, shall humble themselves, and pray, and seek my face, and turn from their wicked ways; then will I hear from heaven, and will forgive their sin, and will heal their land."*

We can take that lesson straight from Jesus. For it is written, "Curse is anyone hanged on a tree," and while hanging on the cross, Jesus prayed for forgiveness for God's people. Jesus had to be very humble to be crucified by his own people and still ask God to forgive them. If it weren't for Jesus' humility to lay his life down freely, you and I wouldn't have salvation today.

Luke 23:33-34 NLT *33: "When they came to a place called The Skull, they nailed him to the cross. And the criminals were also crucified—one on his right and one on his left. 34 Jesus said, "Father, forgive them, for they don't know what they are doing." And the soldiers gambled for his clothes by throwing dice."*

If white, Black, brown, or whatever skin color has wounded you in any way, Jesus shows us the key to being healed is to forgive them, whether wrong or right! When we pray to God with any bitterness in our heart, not forgiving those we are angry with, we're hindering our own prayers from being answered by God. This hindrance includes any anger toward any race and ethnicity, whether they've drastically hurt us intentionally or unintentionally.

Mark 11:25 ERV, 25: *"When you are praying and you remember that you are angry with another person about something, forgive that person. Forgive them so that your Father in heaven will also forgive your sins."*

→Next is to ask God for His peace.

Scripture mentions a peace from God that surpasses all our understanding of what is right, wrong, justified, or not. This peace comes with prayer and thanksgiving. We ask for His peace, but when we pray and petition with a heart and spirit of thanksgiving, then comes God's peace that we may never quite understand or make sense of, but it's there.

Philippians 4:6-7, *"Don't worry about anything; instead, pray about everything. Tell God what you need and thank him for all he has done. Then, you will experience God's peace, which exceeds anything we can understand. His peace will guard your hearts and minds as you live in Christ Jesus."*

Applying God's Word

God's Word is the answer to everything. Everything we ever need is in the Word of God, even healing our racial wounds and historical racial trauma: massacres, plagues, slavery, conquests, ethnic-origin issues, etc. We must surrender to a life of Christ and become Christ-minded to see the fruits of inner healing work in our lives and others.

Jesus was privileged. He sat at the Father's right hand in such a perfect position. God saw sin, left his position at the right hand, and became flesh to save us sinners. Wow! Only if we could have more Jesus in the land with people who have privilege, people whose voices are heard, who can be a part of the solution, helping others get free from the world's problems would be ideal.

As Believers, God has given us power and authority to help and fight for those less fortunate than us. Yet, many still don't. Is it fear? Is it ignorance? Do we believe we have a chance or that it's our responsibility? Well, it is. Jesus stood as a proxy for our sins to bear it all, bringing salvation, healing, and freedom to God's people. What does stand proxy mean?

"Standing proxy" *is the act or practice of a person serving as an authorized* *agent or substitute for another* —used mainly in the phrase by proxy. 2a: authority or power to act for another. Jesus stood in the gap for us to access God's throne. There's a saying that says hate the sin, not the sinner. Well, I pose another challenge for us: hate the devil and not the slave owner. Hate the devil and not the police officer who kills the innocent Black and Brown. Hate the devil and not the racists. There is someone to hate, but it's not people. It is the devil.

Believers, we must know access is here! God has given us a multitude of His sons and daughters from every race, creed, and nationality to stand proxy, authorizing the power of forgiveness and healing through faith. This is done by an authorized person representing the person from the race or person of color who hurt you and is committed to understanding and apologizing for what was done to the person. Having an emotional support person in your life helps heal the racial wounds in one's life.

How do we see the light we wish to be in the world?

By being an ANTHEM.

The scripture in **Romans 15:3- 6, 3-6,** *"That's exactly what Jesus did.* *He didn't make it easy for himself by avoiding people's troubles but waded* *right in and helped out. "I took on the troubles of the troubled," is the way* *Scripture puts it. Even if it was written in scripture long ago, you can be sure* *it's written for us. God wants the combination of his steady, constant calling* *and warm, personal counsel in scripture to come to characterize us, keeping* *us alert for whatever he will do next. May our dependably steady and warmly* *personal God develop maturity in you so that you have a good relationship* *with each other as well as Jesus has a good relationship with us all. Then we'll* *be a choir—not our voices only, but our very lives singing in harmony in a* *stunning anthem to the God and Father of our Master Jesus!"*

If we love God, then we love God's people…all of them, those who look like us and those who don't. Racism is not of God, nor is it from God, but God is the one who can heal us from it when we recognize, release, and renew our minds.

Romans 12:2 NIV, *"Do not conform to the pattern of this world, but be transformed by the renewing of your mind. Then you will be able to test and approve what God's will is—his good, pleasing and perfect will."*

Glossary Terms and Facts about Racism

Black Wall Street in Tulsa, OK

On May 31 and June 1, 1921, mobs of white residents attacked Black residents, homes, and businesses, as well as cultural and public institutions in the Greenwood District of Tulsa, OK, an oil boom city. Greenwood was also known as "Black Wall Street," one of the wealthiest Black communities in the United States. As a result of this attack, thirty-five blocks were systematically looted and burned, destroying 190 businesses and leaving 10,000 people homeless. The property loss estimated by the Tulsa Real Estate Exchange was the equivalent of $31 million in 2017, likely an underestimation.[1]

The Civil Rights Act of 1964: A Long Struggle for Freedom.

(Pub.L. 88–352, 78 Stat. 241, enacted July 2, 1964) is a landmark civil rights and labor law in the United States that outlaws discrimination based on race, color, religion, sex, and national origin. It prohibits unequal application of voter registration requirements, racial segregation in schools and public accommodations, and employment discrimination. The act "remains one of the most significant legislative achievements in American history."

Colorblindness

Colorblindness is the racial ideology that posits the best way to end discrimination is by treating individuals as equally as possible, without regard to race, culture, or ethnicity. This belief dismisses the lived experiences of people of color but also suggests that racism does not exist so long as one ignores it. The word "blind" means not being able to see. This means that in terms of racial colorblindness, a person is also choosing to not just see race or skin color, but also the racial disparities, inequities, history of violence, and current trauma perpetuated within a racist society.[2]

Colorism

Discrimination based on skin color, also known as colorism or shadeism, is a form of prejudice and/or discrimination in which people who share similar ethnic traits or perceived race are treated differently based on the social implications that come with the cultural meanings that are attached to skin color.

Research has found extensive evidence of discrimination based on skin color in criminal justice, business, the economy, housing, health care, media, and politics in the United States and Europe. Lighter skin tones are seen as preferable in many countries in Africa, Asia, and South America.

Emmett Till Antilynching Law

is a United States landmark federal law that makes lynching a federal hate crime after a century of proposed efforts named after the 1955 lynching of 14-year-old Emmett Till in Mississippi, which sparked national and international outrage.

The act amends Matthew Shepard and James Byrd Jr.'s Hate Crimes Prevention Act and prior hate crime laws to define lynching as any conspired bias-motivated offense that results in death or serious bodily injury. It was passed by the U.S House of Representatives on February 28, 2022, and the U.S. Senate on March 7, 2022, and signed into law on March 29, 2022, by President Joe Biden.[3]

Jim Crow Law

Laws that discriminated against black Americans by requiring segregation -- for example, in public schools, public places, and public transportation. "Jim Crow" was a derogatory term for black Americans, most likely derived from "Jump Jim Crow," a caricature performed in blackface as early as 1832. Jim Crow laws were declared unconstitutional and put to an end during the Civil Rights Movement in the 1960s.

Privilege

According to the Cambridge Dictionary, the term 'privilege' refers to "an unearned advantage or entitlement that only one person or group of people has, usually because of their position or because they are rich." This is often attributed to *dominant social groups* which refers to groups that control the value systems and rewards in a particular society. It can refer to groups who hold political power in society, as well as groups who are of the ethnic or religious majority in a society.

White privilege is a combination of the terms, 'white' and 'privilege'. White privilege can be defined as the implicit societal advantages afforded to White people relative to those who experience racism. According to Francis Kendall, "White privilege is an institutional (rather than personal) set of benefits granted to those of us who, by race, resemble the people who dominate the powerful positions in our institutions." It is the absence of suspicion, prejudice, and other negative behaviors that people who are objects of racism experience. Note that this term does not apply in countries where White people do not make up the majority of the population or the political power in charge, for example, China or Japan.

In order to be more aware of privilege, it is important to think about what it is to see society systemically and structurally instead of only in terms of individuals making individual choices. Once this is realized, it is much easier to identify individuals who, due to their privilege, are granted unearned advantages within this system. When a social, political system, or institution grants privileges and unearned advantages to people who make up the majority of the population or represent those in political power, this is known as *institutional racism.*

It is important to note that having white privilege does not automatically make you racist. It is important to identify these inherent advantages in order to reject them so that they do not continue to reinforce our present hierarchies.

- You must use your voice
- Recognize your privilege

- Educate yourself to be a better advocate
- Check-in and speak up to show you care and are aware of what's going on to make a difference
- Understand that your silence is complicit

Redlining

Redlining is an illegal, discriminatory practice in which a mortgage lender denies loans or an insurance provider restricts services to certain areas of a community, often because of the racial characteristics of the applicant's neighborhood. Legislative action. In the United States, the Fair Housing Act of 1968 was passed to fight the practice of redlining. After the signing of The Civil Rights Act of 1968, also known as The Fair Housing Act, it became unlawful to refuse to rent, sell, or provide financing for a dwelling based on race, religion, and national origin. The 1977 Community Reinvestment Act further outlawed redlining.

Slavery

Slavery is a condition in which another owns one human being. A slave was considered by law as property, or chattel, and was deprived of most of the rights ordinarily held by free persons. Passed by Congress on January 31, 1865, and ratified on December 6, 1865, the 13th Amendment abolished slavery in the United States and provides that "Neither slavery nor involuntary servitude, except as a punishment for crime whereof the party shall have been duly convicted, shall exist within the United States

Peter Scazzero, pastor of New Life Fellowship in Queens, New York, developed what he calls *The Racism/Bridge Builder Test*.

Here is a test created by Pastor Peter Scazzero to help Christians see if they are racially biased and/or a Christian Racist:

1. Is there a particular group of people/ethnicity/race that you simply can't stand?

2. Is there any particular group of people/ethnicity/race that you wished your child wouldn't marry? Or you wouldn't marry?

3. Are there types of people who cause you to cross the street if you are walking alone?

4. Does anything happen inside you when you see interracial couples? What types or combinations of couples?

5. When was the last time you visited inside the home or apartment of someone from a different culture or race? When was the last time you invited them to your home or apartment?

6. What is your attitude towards people/groups whose musical preferences are different from yours? (e.g. Classical, classic rock, hard rock, Pop, Jazz, Hip-Hop, R and B (rhythm and blues), gospel, heavy metal, etc.

7. What type of person would you most trust to invest or steward your money? What type of person would you least trust to invest or steward your money?

8. When you meet people from another race/culture who do not fit your stereotype (i.e. nicer, smarter, dumber, aggressive, passive, and/or more articulate) than you expected, are you surprised?

9. When a driver of a different ethnicity/race than yours drives their car too fast or too slow or makes a mistake, do you say to yourself, "Well, that figures!"

"**YOU MUST** *confront* it, *address* it, and hand it /" *over!*

CHAPTER 8

IDENTIFYING EMOTIONAL WOUNDS AND DEFENSE MECHANISMS

The goal of this teaching is not to forget those hurtful events or trauma, but to receive healing for them. Holy Spirit can and will remove the sting so that when you look back on a healed wound, you see it differently because it has been healed and is no longer painful to remember. Remember what Dr. David Seamands said, *"People will continue to respond to their wounds, and those scars will manifest themselves through deep character and interpersonal flaws until they are confronted, addressed, and handed over to Jesus!"* You must confront it, address it, and hand it over!

The first thing we need to do is identify the problem and realize the need for inner healing. Below is a list of common symptoms to look for in somebody who has an emotional wound:

Inner rawness: there is often a sense of inner rawness and hurt that does not seem to disappear.

Irritability: it is easy to become irritable with others, even if they are not doing anything wrong.

Little or no tolerance: there is a low tolerance issue with others, where we expect and demand from them.

Feelings are constantly rising: anger, hate, resentment, etc., seem to "rise up" within us at the slightest offense from others.

Overly sensitive about an event in your past: if events in your past cause you to become sensitive, angry, or even cause you to lash out, then it is likely revealing a deep emotional wound tied in with that event or memory.

Hard to forgive: it becomes difficult, if not impossible, to love and forgive others. It can also be hard to forgive and love yourself. It can even be challenging to forgive and love God, even though He has done nothing wrong against you!

Hard feeling loved: it is hard to see clearly and realize the love of others and God in your life. You may be surrounded by people who love you, but fully feeling and receiving that love can be difficult. There is a wall that blocks the flow of love into your life. (Remember that wall at the beginning of this curriculum?)

Lashing out: when there is an inner wound that has festered, it becomes easy to lash out or have sudden outbursts of anger, hate, resentment, etc. You may find it easy to lash out at people who love you and have done you no harm.

Feelings of anger towards God: when you are wounded, it is easy to blame God for your troubles and hardships. Blaming God is the last thing you want to do when seeking inner healing because it virtually puts a wall in your mind that can block the healing power of the Holy Spirit. Although He desires to heal your wounds, He will not override your free will, and if you hold hate in your heart against Him, it can block His efforts to heal your wounds.

Self-hate: when you suffer hurt from past abuse, you begin to think that perhaps what happened to you was deserved because of something you did. This thought is not valid. Abuse is never acceptable, even if a child is being out of order. Parental love disciplines and corrects, but never abuses.

Easily frustrated: because of the inner turmoil that an inner wound causes, it is easy to become frustrated with everyday chores and responsibilities.

Escapism: as a result of inner turmoil, it is easy to want to escape or suppress reality. Escaping can be in the form of overeating, drinking, smoking, porn, spending binges, etc. When we indulge in escapism, addictions can form and open the door to spirits of addiction, which makes the addictions virtually impossible to break.

Cutting: usually, a person who cuts themselves has an alter-ego inside and is holding much pain and needs to release that pain, or they honestly feel that they deserve the pain (self-hate/religious bondage).

Retaliation urges: because of built-up hate and anger due to unforgiveness, if we have a festering inner wound, we will find it easy to retaliate or snap back at those who offend us or step on our toes.

Irresponsible behavior: inner pain can consume a person's mind and can eventually take on a careless approach to life. It is hard to feel good about ourselves if we have an inner wound, and if we do not feel good about ourselves, it will begin to show in our lifestyle.

Irrational expectations of others: we, who have been wounded, may set high expectations for those around us. Others ought to hold unrealistic standards and be very intolerant of any mistakes made. We find it hard to forbear (put up with) one another as the Bible commands us. (see Colossians 3:13).

Perfectionism: a person who has an emotional wound may also be performance-driven. Perhaps you feel like no matter what you did, you could never please a parent or authority figure. Later in life, that "rejection wound" causes you to be a performer to the point that you are never satisfied and burned out by your efforts.

Feelings of hopelessness: This is a typical result of unresolved inner wounds. Since God's love is blocked in your life, it becomes difficult to see why He would love or care for you, and therefore, you become an easy target for feelings of hopelessness.

Drivenness: when you suffer from an emotional wound, it can create a void in your life's meaning, thus driving you to find meaning, purpose, and happiness. This drive could be in college degrees, careers, financial success, etc. Instead of appreciating the person God has made us to be, we chase what we believe will bring true happiness and purpose to our lives.

Obsessive-Compulsive Disorder or OCD: Obsessive-Compulsive Disorder (OCD) often involves emotional wounds that were never healed. It is not a mental disorder or disease. It is a "spiritually rooted bondage" in the person's mind that needs to be uprooted. This disorder is especially true with people who have bondages to self-hate, self-resentment, self-unforgiveness, etc., basically demonic torment brought on by a person's bondages to fear and shame. Those affected may experience thoughts being 'pushed' through their mind that they would usually never think (completely against their true nature), or they may experience a strong pulling on their thoughts in a specific direction. They may even hear voices inside their mind or, in some other way, sense that something is wrong. A terrific way to describe it is to imagine a magnet in your mind pulling your thoughts in a specific direction even though you hate those thoughts. It feels like you are sharing your mind with another spirit you completely disagree with.

Hostility towards God, self, and others: You tend to feel hostile towards God or others because of bound-up emotions. This emotion is usually rooted in bitterness against God for not preventing something from happening to you, bitterness against somebody who has wronged or harmed you emotionally, or bitterness against yourself for failures into which you have fallen.

Defense Mechanisms

Many people do not realize it, but they have defense mechanisms preventing their emotional wounds from healing. Holy Spirit is eager and ready to heal you, but when you do not receive it, there is a reason something is blocking or hindering that healing from manifesting. All too often, that reason is a defense mechanism serving as a wall or blockage that prevents or hinders the light of Christ from penetrating and healing the wound in you.

Once Satan has that "wound" in you, he wants to ensure that it does not heal. That is where he works hand-in-hand with fleshly defense mechanisms to keep your wound from ever healing.

What is a defense mechanism? A defense mechanism is an ungodly reaction in a person that is designed to prevent a person from further harm. It can be fear, unforgiveness, rebellion, etc. Think of it as a wall that keeps out the bad and good guys.

Defense mechanisms are rooted in your human flesh and are inclined not to trust God. That is why a defense mechanism can cause a person to find it challenging to trust God. Instead, we would act upon our fears or unforgiveness to protect us rather than lay our burdens and concerns before Jesus' feet and trust Him to care for them. In reality, defense mechanisms are fleshly ways of dealing with and handling things God has told us to trust Him.

How do we recognize a defense mechanism? Be watchful for emotions that tend to "rise up" within you when faced with situations that put you at risk of being re-hurt in a particular area of your life. Defense mechanisms can come in various forms, but the two main categories involve fear and unforgiveness. Fear is afraid of being hurt, and unforgiveness says, "I will not allow myself to be hurt."

Unforgiveness and *fear* both have children. Unforgiveness is the root that leads to resentment, anger, hate, and even murder. Fear has a family all on its own, including fear, worry, insecurity, dread, panic, etc. Fear is just as much of a defense mechanism as unforgiveness.

If you struggle with issues of anger, rebellion (blaming others), resentment (rooted in unforgiveness), and so forth, then you are up against a defense mechanism. A defense mechanism will rise when it perceives potential harm in an area of a person's life.

Understanding defense mechanisms

Defense mechanisms are usually there because a person (you) has been abused, hurt, etc. All these mechanisms know is hurt and pain, so they take it upon themselves to protect the person from further pain. Some people will even vow, "I will never let anybody get close to me again!" Such vows bind a person's soul and invite demonic bondage. Demons are more than eager to work alongside defense mechanisms to create bondages with anger, resentment, fear, and so forth. In such cases, the defense mechanisms must be addressed, and the emotional damage must be healed. Now, not only do you have a defense mechanism, but you also have an inner vow.

Where there is self-pity, there is usually a root of rejection that creates a defense mechanism where one holds onto their hurt and pain when looking for love and acceptance from others. Someone who has built defense mechanisms will often find it difficult to talk about certain things or receive correction about their attitude or conduct. A feeling of "Don't go there!" usually rises within the person. They want to avoid addressing the root as if it were poison, believing their defense mechanisms are protecting them from further damage to themselves.

Tearing down defense mechanisms

It is essential to realize that defense mechanisms will attempt to put up a roadblock to outsiders, regardless of whether it further harms the healing power of Jesus. This roadblock will prevent Jesus from even reaching the wound to be healed. We must make way for God to heal the wound! Listed below are the roadblocks one needs to tear down so they can pull up their roots and Jesus can heal their wounds:

Roadblock #1: Unthankfulness. Defense mechanisms are there because of pain and hurt, and they come from a place of unthankfulness. Thankfulness is an essential key to receiving healing for damaged emotions. Stop dwelling on what was done to you and all of the fleshly reasons why you are unthankful and begin to dwell upon the things that God has given you.

Roadblock #2: Blaming others (including yourself and God). Defense mechanisms cause you to blame yourself, others, or God for what happened. Blaming yourself opens you up to bondages of self-hate, self-resentment, self-unforgiveness, self-rejection, etc. Regardless of who your defense mechanism is blaming, it is enforcing a wall that is blocking your healing. It is keeping your eyes on the problem and off of Christ, who provided the solution for you. It is of the utmost importance that you accept personal responsibility for your ungodly and hateful reactions within your heart.

Roadblock #3: Fear. When the defense mechanisms make you afraid of being hurt again, you operate out of fear. This fear will cause you to dodge situations that may expose you to further pain, rejection, etc. God's Word tells you to cast all of your fears upon Him, for He cares for you (see 1 John 4:18). When you don't know the love of God, it will make it difficult to trust Him. It is difficult, if not impossible, to trust somebody when we do not know who loves and cares for us. Therefore, an essential key to overcoming these fears is to learn of the love of God for you and meditate on His goodness. Fear also draws you inward, making you dysfunctional in genuine relationship building and even rendering you useless ministering to others.

Roadblock #4: Unforgiveness. We will deal with Unforgiveness in great depth later in this, but the issue with unforgiveness is rooted in a distrust of God's justice. When you refuse to forgive, you are afraid that nobody else (including God) will do anything about the wrong that was done against you. Therefore, you will hold onto it and see that the person receives justice (in their heart). You do not believe that God is going to ensure that justice happens. Forgiveness is trusting God to handle the situation and bring justice. Did you know that you can prevent a person from receiving justice? It's true. If you fail to give Him that place, you cannot expect Him to act on your behalf and bring justice.

Romans 12:19 tells us, *"Dearly beloved, avenge not yourselves, but rather give place unto wrath: for it is written, Vengeance is mine; I will repay, saith the Lord."*

One key to living a life of forgiveness is believing in your spirit that God cares for you and everything that was done and said against you. As we trust Him, justice will be brought to those who wronged us.

Roadblock #5: Incorrect perceptions. A critical key to inner healing is tearing down strongholds, which are incorrect thinking patterns or perceptions that have been burned into our mindsets. When you perceive God as a cruel, distant, and unloving taskmaster, then it makes it difficult for you to trust Him and cast your cares upon Him. When you perceive that you are dirty and have shameful failures, then you will not be confident in your relationship with God, and your faith will be severely damaged. You will draw away from Him rather than to Him, and that's where the flow of healing is.

A Word about Trust vs. Forgiveness

Trust and forgiveness are misunderstood and often confused as being the same. That is not true. Extending forgiveness is always required of you. Remember the scripture in Matthew 6:14-15, but trusting the person who has offended you is another story. Let's say that you were raped or abused physically, mentally, or even spiritually by a church or pastor; it is vital to forgive that person who has done this terrible thing to you, but it may also be very unwise to allow yourself to be alone with them again thus putting you in harm's way.

While you do not have to trust others who have harmed you, you do need to trust God in every area of life. Trusting God requires a knowledge of His love. The Word tells us that perfect love casts out all fear. Why? Because when you know His love, it is a cinch to trust Him in every area of your life! Another factor that hinders your ability to trust God is not feeling confident about your relationship with Him. Many Christians are plagued with guilt, shame, and feelings of condemnation. Somehow, the devil tries to make you think that your failures are more significant than the Blood of Jesus, which was shed for the removal of your sins. Are you problem-focused on your sin and failures or solution-focused on what Jesus did about it? Is the Blood of Jesus, which was shed for the sins of the whole world, so weak that it cannot wipe away the failures in your life? If that is what you are thinking, then you are grossly underestimating the value and power of the Blood of Jesus!

Prayer for Defense Mechanisms

Once you've decided to get rid of your defense mechanisms, verbally confess your choice to tear down ungodly defense mechanisms by reciting the prayer below:

"Holy Spirit, I now pull down the ungodly walls and defense mechanisms I created, believing they were there to protect me. I know I can do all things through Christ, who strengthens me and can endure whatever is necessary that lies before me because Jesus was crucified for my sins, and the price is paid. I choose to no longer hold on to the hurt and accept it. I choose to no longer walk in fear and blame others for what happened to me. I walk in forgiveness and pray for a grateful heart, thanking Jesus for healing me. I stand boldly on God's Word, knowing I am free because of the blood and sacrifice of Jesus Christ, and these defense mechanisms shall never return. Amen."

" Satan CANNOT stand *humility* because it BREAKS his power *over* YOU, but *God loves it!* "

CHAPTER 9

STRONGHOLDS

For though we live in the world, we do not wage war as the world does. The weapons we fight with are not the weapons of the world. On the contrary, they have divine power to demolish strongholds. We demolish arguments and every pretension that sets itself up against the knowledge of God, and we take captive every thought to make it obedient to Christ.

2 Corinthians 10:3-5

What is a stronghold and why are they important in literal warfare?

A stronghold can be defined as "an ingrained repetitive thinking process which your mind regularly travels down." What you "think" determines how you see yourself, others, and the world. Your beliefs determine what you feel, and how you feel motivates you to do. Even though you cannot change your feelings, you can change your belief system. The Spirit of God wants each of you to capture any demonic strongholds that hold you captive and strengthen the stronghold of the Holy Spirit in you.

Now, these fighting words below are metaphorical. They speak of weapons, strongholds, high things, and bringing into captivity, yet these are not carnal or worldly weapons but *spiritual ones*; not strongholds of stone but of *imaginations* or *arguments*; not high things in high towers but *highfalutin attitudes;* not taking into captivity enemy soldiers but *enemy thoughts.*

A stronghold is a defense structure:

- *Refuge* - shelter or protection in times of trouble
Psalms 9:9, *The LORD is a refuge for the oppressed, a stronghold in times of trouble.*

- *Cliff* - other lofty, high, or inaccessible place, especially to one's enemies. 1 Samuel 23:14, *David stayed in the wilderness strongholds and in the hills of the Desert of Ziph.* Day after day Saul searched for him, but God did not give David into his hands.

- *High fortress, fort, or high tower*
Ps 144:2, *[The LORD is] My lovingkindness and my fortress, My high tower and my deliverer, My shield and the One in whom I take refuge, Who subdues my people under me.*

Why would a "high thing" like to hang out on a high cliff or a high tower, exalting itself? Because it is safe up there. If an enemy comes, it is much easier to drive him away from a stronghold in a high place.

→ *Know This: There is a devil who has a scheme against you.*

According to 2 Cor 2:11, lest Satan should take advantage of us;

for we are not ignorant of his devices.

And Eph 6:11, Put on the whole armor of God,
that you may be able to stand against the wiles of the devil.

Ignoring the devil's scheme will distract you from your divine destiny by giving you an alternative identity and an alternative destiny. It has been proven that your alternate identity probably started operating when you were a child. Maybe the enemy whispered a lie that you embraced to be true. You thought about that lie over and over until it became a normal thought pattern. What you did not realize is that your enemy, the devil, the master schemer, was shaping your thinking as you continued to embrace the lies he "whispered" to your mind. Since you thought those thoughts over and over, the lies became truth to you. And once they feel like the truth, they become part of your identity. You have now embraced an alternative identity that actually feels like the "real you." In reality, it is a counterfeit from the devil or master schemer to derail you from your true divine destiny and prevent you from becoming the very person that God intended you to be. Going through those alternative thought patterns repetitively establishes them in your mind like the ruts and grooves on an old dirt road. You go down those "thought patterns" until you wear grooves and deep ruts. If you have ever gone down an old dirt road that has been traveled heavily, you know what I am talking about.

How to Capture a Stronghold

You must know that if you continue those thought patterns long enough and wear those grooves and ruts in your mind, those faulty pathways become your default thinking- or where you naturally gravitate if left unchecked. Most default thinking patterns are based on lies and become ungodly strongholds that RULE your life. You then become a slave to your thoughts so that they now control YOU instead of YOU controlling them. That causes an unrighteous thinking process that ends up ruling, controlling, dominating your thoughts, and dictating unrighteous behaviors.

Strongholds are captured by people with grit who are willing to fight.

God knows all about strongholds, and He knows how to take them — and He will tell you how to do it if you are willing to fight! When you come up against a stronghold, do you want to give up? Or are you willing to fight to take the stronghold?

One thing you should remember about a stronghold is that it is a place, not a person. A stronghold is only a threat if there are enemy soldiers inside. Indeed, a stronghold can also be a place of comfort, a safe place. For example, in 2 Samuel 22:2-3, David said:

> The LORD is my rock, my fortress, and my deliverer; my God is my rock, in whom I take refuge, *my shield, and the horn of my salvation. He is my stronghold, my refuge, and my savior from violent men you save me.*

The person or persons inside the stronghold could be your enemy or your friend. In a spiritual stronghold, there could be demons or the Holy Spirit. But just as a physical stronghold is not an enemy soldier, nor is a spiritual stronghold a demon. A spiritual stronghold is a *habitual pattern of thought* built into one's thought life. Satan wants to capture your mind: the mind is the citadel of the soul. A citadel was used in times of war to protect a garrison or political power from the inhabitants of the town where it was located, designed to ensure loyalty from the town they defended.

Remember: He who controls the mind controls a very strategic place!

Romans 8:5-6: *Those who live according to the sinful nature have their minds set on what that nature desires; but those who live in accordance with the Spirit have their minds set on what the Spirit desires. The mind of sinful man is death, but the mind controlled by the Spirit is life and peace.*

In Matt 12:34-35, *He said, For out of the overflow of the heart the mouth speaks. The good man brings good things out of the good stored up in him, and the evil man brings evil things out of the evil stored up in him.*

Strongholds are also storage places, holding food, water, and weapons. A stronghold strengthens as more stuff—more thoughts—gets stored there. In the life of a mind, the things you were once aware of get stored in the unconscious memory, but it can make a stronghold a tough nut to crack! A stronghold is a way of thinking and feeling that has developed a life of its own in a person. It might be a rut of depression, recurring unbelief, or habitually bad temper. Those were all strongholds in my life, but with God's help, not anymore! It might be a repeating pattern of failure. Sometimes, a stronghold will cause you to provoke others to reject you without necessarily knowing you are doing it. It might be a stronghold of resentment or worthlessness. If a child is sexually molested or badly verbally abused, a stronghold of worthlessness may build up a stockpile of negative thoughts. The child is beautiful-and undoubtedly beautiful in the eyes of God; however, a stronghold gives arguments like these:

> ➤ *"I'm guilty."*
> ➤ *"Nobody could really love me."*
> ➤ *"I am worthless."*
> ➤ *"I'm ugly."*
> ➤ *"Nobody would like me if they really got to know me."*
> ➤ *"Nobody understands me."*
> ➤ *"Nobody really cares for me."*
> ➤ *"Nobody wants me for me."*

These thoughts are all a pack of lies, but they can be a stronghold keeping out the truth about God's love. Such a person may hear a message about God's love, whether from a pulpit or a friend, but it goes in one ear and out the other, bouncing off the walls of a stronghold of rejection or worthlessness. You almost hear the truth come to set you free, and then comes another thought:

"Yeah, but what about...?" or "You just don't understand...."

And out comes another string of lies, excuses, and smokescreens, shot down by blocking spirits. Thus, a stronghold creates inner captivity to deception and misery. A stronghold keeps a person from thinking clearly, accepting the truth, repenting sin, and receiving deliverance. It can also keep an unbeliever from hearing the good news or a believer from hearing the fullness of the good news.

Taking Down A Stronghold

First, you must engage in spiritual warfare to tear down and demolish ungodly strongholds. Ungodly strongholds are those ingrained thought patterns that are against the knowledge of God, disobedient thoughts that have not been taken captive. If they are not addressed, those areas will eventually become masters and determine how YOU think and feel. You might succeed in temporarily pushing wrongful thoughts to the back of your mind, but if they are not "dismantled" and removed, they will surface again, and negativity will impact your life again. You have to be able to see a stronghold to know what you are dealing with; otherwise, you will not be able to tear it down. But strongholds of the mind can be hidden—evil things hang out in darkness. Satan is the prince of darkness, but the Messiah is the prince of light. You have been called out of darkness into his marvelous light! Nevertheless, if there is an old, sinful thought pattern, that is a stronghold.

Ephesians 5:11 urges us to *"have nothing to do with the fruitless deeds of darkness, but rather expose them."*

In Psalm 26:2, *David prayed, "Test me, O LORD, and try me, examine my heart and my mind."* Are you willing to let God reveal the strongholds in your life? Then, the first stronghold you may have to start tearing down is pride. Who was the first to be guilty of pride? Satan, and massively so! Pride is the armor Satan uses to keep demonic strongholds hidden on the inside. The spirit of pride keeps people from ever seeing that they are trapped in demonic darkness, but the Spirit of God is determined to bring down the stronghold of pride.

When ungodly strongholds rule your thought life, the structures established will become the support system for the demonic. An ungodly house of thoughts that is built on lies and wounds will attract and shelter demonic spirits. Please know this: Unrighteousness thought systems agree with darkness, and that kind of agreement empowers the devil. Your problem is that you have entertained those thoughts for so long that they feel completely normal,comfortable, and acceptable to you. The old thought patterns must be dismantled, and new thoughts that agree with the Word and your new nature and true destiny must be built.

James 4:7 continues with another promise:

"Submit yourselves, then, to God. Resist the devil, and he will flee from you."

→ Know this: Satan cannot stand humility because it breaks his power over you, but God loves it!

In the book of James, he also states in 4:10, *"Humble yourselves before the Lord, and he will lift you up."*

Once you recognize the stronghold, repentance is the next step to bringing it down. Be honest before God, and humbly let the Spirit expose the stronghold in the darkness. When you gave your heart and life to Jesus, you were made into a new creature right then and there, and you reconnected to God through Holy Spirit. In this divine connection, because of the indwelling of Jesus through the Holy Spirit, you have the mind of Christ. At the beginning of this study, we discussed the importance of having the mind of Christ. We learned that just because it is available does not mean your thoughts are always in tune with His. The renewing of the mind transforms new creation believers. (Rom 12:2). You must pursue the heavenly thinking available to you. Three steps were given to you to renew your mind. It is a daily discipline. Colossians 3:2-3 the scripture says to "set your mind on things above." Yes, there will be a battle, a struggle, even a fight, but if you are obedient and continue to fight this good fight, you must set your mind on things above and believe you WILL win—no doubt about it.

Pray Psalm 26:2: *"Test me, O LORD, and try me, examine my heart and mind."* When Holy Spirit shows you an area of darkness, you repent, regardless of an instinct you might feel telling you to defend yourself. If this is so, silence the little lawyer who steps out of the dark corner of your mind, pleading, "My client is not so bad." If you let him, that whiny defense attorney will defend you just fine, but you will never see what is wrong in you nor face what needs to change.

Who is the best defense attorney of all time? Yeshua! How does He defend you? How does He justify you? By his BLOOD. Therefore, you do not need to explain yourself, but let Jesus do it. When you bring God your broken spirit and remorseful heart, He does not turn away and dislike you.

Psalm 51:17 reads, *My sacrifice, O God, is a broken spirit; a broken and contrite heart you, God, will not despise.*

Suppose a stronghold has gotten extremely entrenched and robust. Sometimes, a frontal attack on a stronghold does not work. What should you do? The Jewish soldiers tried to capture the Old City of Jerusalem with a frontal attack a couple of times in the War of Independence, but as soon as they got up to the gates of the Old City, they were thrown back. Yet, victory was declared for the Jews because they never gave up hope, but innovated new ways and weapons to defeat their enemy, plus get support from other nations.

When we're surrounded by a stronghold of negative thinking consumed with bad and old speculations, we must do what the Jews did: innovate our weapon of warfare. And we do this with the weapon of warfare called "praise." The Bible confirms that singing praises unto the Lord protects us.

Psalms 32:7 states, *"You are my hiding place; you will protect me from trouble and surround me with songs of deliverance."*

Surround the stronghold with praise, singing psalms and spiritual songs to God. Praise is a powerful way to bring down a stronghold; demons can not stand it when we praise God. For every opposing stronghold, there's a powerful way to surround it with the opposite truth from God.

For example:

- If you are struggling with a stronghold of depression, surround it with hope.

- If you are struggling with a stronghold of rejection, surround it with acceptance from God.

- If you struggle with a stronghold of unresolved anger, surround it with forgiveness.

- If you are struggling with a stronghold of fear, surround it with the knowledge of God's love.

- If you are struggling with a stronghold of failure, surround it with the victory of the resurrection!

- If the stronghold is rejection, study all the Bible says about God's acceptance.

Once you've identified a stronghold, go to the Scriptures and study the opposite truth from God with a concordance, chain Bible, or even a topical Bible. Then surround that stronghold with the word of God! Listen, once the enemy sees he is surrounded by humble submission, praise, and the word of God, his resistance will quickly weaken, and he might already be gone.

Prayer Against Strongholds

Dear Heavenly Father, test me, O LORD, and try me, examine my heart and mind. Show me any areas in my life that I have not fully surrendered to you.

(If you recognize any area of chronic sin strengthened by negative thinking, take a moment to confess it to the Lord now.)

Lord, forgive me for any compromise. Give me the courage to pull down every stronghold within me without reluctance or willful deception in my heart. Thank you, Lord Yeshua, for forgiving and cleansing me from all my sins and breaking every curse against me on the cross.

By the power of the Holy Spirit and in the Name of Yeshua, I bind any satanic influences reinforcing compromise and sin within me. I submit myself to the light of the Spirit of Truth to expose any strongholds of sin in me. By the mighty weapons of the Spirit and the Word, I proclaim that each evil stronghold is coming down!

I purpose to surround this evil stronghold with praise and affirming truth from the Word of God. I propose to take every pattern of negative thinking captive and bring it to obedience to the Messiah. By God's grace, I shall follow through until the ruin of this stronghold is removed from my mind!

I stand on God's Word in faith, declaring Philippians 4:8 over my mind to think about whatever is true, whatever is noble, whatever is right, whatever is pure, whatever is lovely, whatever is admirable—if anything is excellent or praiseworthy— I will think about such things. I will talk about such things. I will get involved in such things. By God's grace, I purpose to build up one stronghold within my mind and heart: the stronghold of the living God!

The name of the LORD is a strong tower; the righteous will run to it and be safe." In the shelter of your presence, O God my Savior, you will keep me safe.

In Jesus Name, Amen ✝

<u>Rejection</u>

It is an experience that is so universally understood that it does not even require a definition. You have felt rejected. I have felt rejected. To one degree or another, we all have felt rejected and tasted the pain of rejection from others. We can all agree that rejection hurts. Rejection is one of Satan's most effective forms of oppression. Rejection may keep a sinner from coming to God for salvation and a Christian from reaching their full potential in God. Rejection undermines, breaks, and prevents normal and harmonious relations between family members, marriage partners, fellow workers, and friends. It also distorts your image of God as a loving heavenly Father who loves you and wants only the best for you.

Being denied love is at the root of rejection. Rejection, whether active, passive, accurate, or imaginary, robs Jesus Christ of His rightful position as Lord in the lives of His children and keeps believers from experiencing the vitality and quality of life He alone can give. Rejection results in wounding of the heart—sometimes so painful that the mind refuses to deal with it, so we bury it in our subconscious. Later, it surfaces in other ways and causes us problems. Rejection is the greatest undiagnosed and untreated malady within the Body of Christ today. Regrettably, most of those coming for prayer suffer from feelings of rejection.

Symptoms of Rejection

Below are examples of rejection displayed in one's life. Go through the list and see if you can identify with any symptoms. Ask yourself, "Is this how I feel about myself?"

- low self-image, insecure, withdrawn personality
- self-condemning, self-hate, try to please others
- worthless, believe I am a failure, agony within
- inferior, question my identity, display a facade
- starved for love, promiscuous, cannot love spouse
- unworthy, fear of rejection, not knowing who I am
- approval-seeking, self-rejecting, feeling abandoned

- self-accusing, can't accept love, depressed
- can't give love, internal hurt/pain
- no lasting relationships, earn acceptance by being good or by hard work

Root Causes of Rejection

The root causes of rejection can be found from one or more of several sources, which are listed below:

- Heritage rejection
- Generational rejection
- Rejection after birth
- Symptoms of rejection after birth
- Being an adopted child, or forced either to live with relatives or in a foster home, or to live in a different culture
- Healing from the effects of adoption
- Factors that cause rejection during early childhood
- Problems in school caused by teachers or schoolmates (that cause rejection)
- Multiple causes of rejection later in life
- Factors that cause rejection within a marriage

Factors that cause rejection during early childhood

Early childhood rejection is the most critical type of rejection that requires inner healing more than the rest because it can involve many factors, including: rejection after birth (including parents, siblings, or other family members), rejection from adoption or foster care, and rejection from teachers or schoolmates. What happens to you as a child is significant in how deeply you struggle with the spirit of rejection lies. See if you identify with any examples below within your life:

- Children who are criticized, over-disciplined, victimized, ignored, or treated as a favorite or who share a family with a sister or brother who is the favorite.

- Parents who persistently confront one another in front of their children;

- Talk of separation or divorce, which may result in the child blaming themselves for causing their parent's problems;

- Parents who only speak to one another through the children;

- A stern, legalistic, or over-disciplinarian father;

- Fathers who are weak-willed, apathetic, or dominated by their wives;

- An alcoholic father or mother;

- Having a sick brother or sister who requires more attention;

- Hearing comments that hurt (for example, "I never wanted you in the first place" or "You are stupid.") Physical, mental, verbal, or sexual abuse occurring through parents, friends, or others who frequent the home environment;

- A child being falsely accused of something done by a brother or sister, etc. (a trust issue develops);

- The conviction or jailing of a close family member;

- A sudden fall in the family's living standards—caused by the unemployment of the family breadwinner, bankruptcy, etc.;

- Experiencing extended periods of loneliness because of parental disinterest;

- The absence of the parents from the child's school or extra-curricular activities;

- Sickness;

- An overload of home responsibilities;

- Severe or cruel punishment;

- One or both parents wanted a child of the opposite sex.

Multi-faceted Spirit of Rejection

Seldom will you find a spirit of rejection present by itself. It is usually accompanied by one or more of the spirits of self-rejection, fear of rejection, fear of abandonment, anxiety, and perceived rejection. In many cases, the seeker has rejected their parents, others, themselves, and God for not doing something to protect them from the hurt and pain they had earlier experienced. The wounded seeker constructs emotional walls around their heart and typically makes inner vows, such as "No one will ever hurt me again." Those who suffer the worst types of rejection at times develop multiple personalities or alter egos as a form of emotional protection. Rejection affects us more profoundly than we care to admit!

The outward expressions or symptoms of rejection and related spirits result in one of two significant areas of response:

(1) an aggressive response - which exhibits rebelliousness, sexual promiscuity, self-sufficiency, anger, rejection of others, deception, and defiance

or

(2) a passive response exhibiting an approval-seeking nature, submissiveness, loneliness, and depression.

The opposite of "reject" is "accept." In God's Word, it confirms,

"He hath made us accepted in the beloved" Ephesians 1:6.

In the Greek, the word "accepted" (as used here) means "highly favored one." When we come to God through Jesus, we are accepted and are as highly favored as Jesus. For further study regarding rejection, read and consider the following scriptures: *Ps. 22:9, 27:10, 29:9-10, 68:5-6, 127:3-5, 139:13-16 and 23-24, Jer. 1:5, Eph. 2:10.*

Even though you may have suffered rejection, you are still accountable for the fruits, i.e., how you have handled, dealt with, and expressed their rejection in anger, rudeness, rebellion, self-pity, etc. These detrimental behaviors must be confessed, and forgiveness from God must be asked for. You need to read truths about yourself and renounce the lies you have previously believed. *Verbally* commit to a conscious decision to eliminate the "bad fruit" that rejection has produced in your life, such as: bitterness, resentment, hatred, and rebellion. *Verbally* accept yourself, as hard as that may be. Look in the mirror and tell yourself that you are God's workmanship and have no right to criticize what God has made.

Ephesians 2:10, *For we are His workmanship, created in Christ Jesus for good works, which God prepared beforehand that we should walk in them.*

Did you know that if you are bound in chains of rejection and abandonment, you might not even know what binds you? True story. The enemy does not want you to see if you have a stronghold of rejection, so he will try to keep his dirty work hidden in webs and shadows. However, our God is much greater, and Holy Spirit will reveal any stronghold of rejection and abandonment in your life. All you have to do is ask Him and listen.

That revelation might come any number of ways. For example, the Lord might give you profound revelation about this subject while you are reading His Word one day. So, what does the stronghold of rejection and abandonment look like? Let us look at how this evil manifests in your life. Of course, every person is different, but the manifestations of this evil stronghold are pretty consistent, in my experience, anyway.

4 Signs You Have a Stronghold of Rejection and Abandonment:

1. You isolate yourself.

Whether you tell yourself that you are doing it for a good reason or not, self-isolation is always the work of the enemy. God's people are made to be one body, tightly joined and knit together. We are spiritually dependent upon one another. And if you break away from covenant fellowship with your brothers and sisters in Christ, it is easy for the enemy to pick you off.

2. You believe that God has rejected you.

Nothing could be further than the truth. The Bible says that it is not God's will that ANY should perish, but that ALL should come to repentance.

II Peter 3:8-9 says, *"But, beloved, do not forget this one thing, that with the Lord one day is as a thousand years, and a thousand years as one day. The Lord is not slack concerning His promise, as some count slackness, but is longsuffering toward us, not willing that any should perish but that all should come to repentance."*

God has NOT rejected you!! He earnestly desires to be in an intimate relationship with you. However, the enemy will tell you the opposite. The *devil will twist things in your mind if you let him*, deceiving you into thinking that you are so grand in your badness that you are above God's mercy and above the ability of the blood of Jesus to save. Our own hurt gets in the way of understanding just how much He loves us and has not rejected us, but reading God's word helps us renew our minds.

Romans 12:2 says, *"Do not conform to the pattern of this world, but be transformed by the renewing of your mind. Then you will be able to test and approve what God's will is—his good, pleasing and perfect will."*

The enemy uses his evil web of tricks and lies, including a spirit of pride plus the leviathan spirit to twist the truth in your mind when a door has been opened. The leviathan represents the forces of chaos. It keeps confusion going all the time and cannot stand for there to be peace. Of course, this is still no match for the power of God. The leviathan spirit is a metaphorical reference scripture draws from the image of a tremendous serpentine sea creature. See **Psalms 74** It describes a spirit that works to twist words and perceptions to disrupt and destroy the people of God. Recently, Leviathan has worked in the body of Christ, including government and society. People with leviathan spirits are proud, haughty, arrogant, and refuse correction. Much damage is done wherever this spirit is not identified and effectively resisted, but don't believe it.

3. Refusing to allow others to see or share in something near and dear to your heart.

For example, maybe you paint terrific pictures but will not let anyone see them. Perhaps you have a beautiful voice and love to sing, but you do not want to let anyone hear you sing. Or you dream of writing a blog that encourages people but is afraid to be transparent and tell people about your life experiences.

What is the common thread in all these situations? Usually, it is *rejection*.

-->How does rejection keep you from sharing your skills and dreams with the world?

Rejection will tell you " they will reject you if you share your gift, heart, idea, skills, or calling with others." They will make fun of you. This demonic spirit will tell you that the people who see these deep things in your heart will reject your dream, laugh at your dream, fail to believe in your dream, etc. And since these dreams and passions are so close to you- so near and dear to your heart–then the idea of anyone rejecting them makes you bleed on the inside, even if nobody has rejected you in that area yet or ever! Isn't that horrible? It is another part of the enemy's insidious tactic to steal, rob, kill, and destroy both you and your destiny in Christ. Ugh.

Interestingly enough, you know someone is starting to heal from rejection and abandonment when they open up and share the deep things in their heart. If someone who has struggled with rejection suddenly opens up and shares something personal, cherish it. Treasure it and know that their opening up means God is healing their heart.

4. You fear that people will reject or abandon you.

A spirit of fear can only come in when you do not know you are loved.

> 1 John 4:18 tells us, *"There is no fear in love; but perfect love casts out fear, because fear involves torment. But he who fears has not been made perfect in love."*

Unfortunately, when people abandon or reject you–or when you believe that they will; then you usually do not know that you are loved. And when you do not know how much Father God loves you, a spirit of fear comes and torments you. But suffice it to say that ongoing fear is concrete evidence that you have not yet been made perfect in love. And the enemy, who hates you and does not play fair at all, sends the spirit of fear to torment you if there is any area in which you do not know you are loved, including if you have suffered through abandonment and rejection. You could be afraid of many different things, but the point here is that the spirit of fear nests on top of abandonment and rejection every time.

Before you begin reading further, take a moment to say this prayer.

Father, I ask that you reveal to me any places in my family lines that need further prayer to break the bondage of sin and ignorance and to restore myself and others to our rightful heritage in you. Look upon all of the people in my generational lines with compassion. Free them all so they may come before you with the true knowledge of your love and forgiveness. Send into every dark and hurting place the love of your Son Jesus Christ that those in the past, present, and future generations may learn to live in the wholeness of body, mind, and spirit to the eternal glory of your holy name, in and through our Lord Jesus Christ. I ask this in Jesus' worthy name. AMEN

Generational Rejection and Curses

We know that all of Adam and Cain's descendants are predisposed to heritage rejection. However, not all persons inherit a spirit of rejection. Abel's sacrifices were acceptable to the Lord. Many curses are conditional. When we are disobedient, the promised curses come upon us (Deut. 28 and 30). Cain received a curse of rejection because of potential heritage rejection and his sins of disobedience and rebellion, while Abel did not.

Generational sin is when our forefathers were disobedient; they incurred a curse, including rejection, and it continues to pass as a curse of rejection upon the heads of the children to the third and fourth generation, as stated in God's word.

Exodus 20:5, *". . . I the Lord thy God am a jealous God, visiting the iniquity of the fathers upon the children unto the third and fourth generation of them that hate me."*

Deuteronomy 5:9, *"...I, the Lord your God, am a jealous God, punishing the children for the sin of the parents to the third and fourth generation of those who hate me,"*

Generational content can show up in many different patterns in families: divorce, alcoholism, depression, addiction, poverty, infidelity, abuse (mental, physical, and verbal), and sexual vices. Anything you notice as a pattern throughout your family could be generational content.

Types of Generational Content

Below are three main types of generational content affecting families—and maybe yours. Each is easily removed through prayer, called "the ripple effect," when a ripple of freedom and healing happens even if you are the only one who prayed. Because of our free will and ability to agree with lies, not every family member will always get healed. Some require personal buy-in and cannot be done for someone else.

Generational Curse

A generational curse is a negative pattern or behavior that is passed down through generations, affecting a person's mind, body, or spirit. Some examples include:

- Addictions: Such as drug or alcohol use, or sex
- Mental illnesses: Such as depression, schizophrenia, or bipolar disorder

These are the lightweights where you will most likely see a ripple through your family. A curse is a declaration spoken over or against your family or done against your family. No one in the family did anything to invite or agree with it, but there is a generation where it seems to have entered the family line. If a family member from three generations ago was addicted to alcohol because of the debilitating depression they dealt with, the generational curse can affect the children. I knew a set of brothers who dealt with alcohol abuse and were also diagnosed with schizophrenia. Both of the sons died alcoholics, and the next generation of boys got hooked on drugs and alcohol which led to their sons struggling with alcohol and depression too. That's three generations of alcohol and mental illness in the family bloodline. In Deuteronomy, it confirms that curses can be passed down to the third and fourth generations and sexual sins affect up to the tenth generation.

In Deuteronomy 23:2 it reads, *"If a person is illegitimate by birth, neither he nor his descendants for ten generations may be admitted to the assembly of the LORD."*

However, the blessing of obedience to God is passed down a thousand generations.

Deuteronomy 7:9 confirms, *Know therefore that the LORD your God is God; he is the faithful God, keeping his covenant of love to a thousand generations of those who love him and keep his commandments.*

Generational Agreement

A generational agreement is the same promise or agreement made with God. For example, God made a promise with Abraham and because God honors His covenants, we as Abraham's seed have the RIGHT to claim and agree that what God promised Abraham we can claim and agree for us for all generations to come.

We see this in Genesis 12:1-3: *"... and you shall be a blessing, I will bless those who bless you, and I will curse those who curse you. And in you all the families of the earth shall be blessed."*

An example of this is someone I personally know. She is a pastor's wife of a large denominational church and because she comes from a family of strong Believers in God---everything her hand touches is blessed. Growing up, she never got into drugs, promiscuous sex, nor dealt with depression, schizophrenia or any bi-polar disorder. God has opened doors for her to share her testimony and speak at multiple events. Her children also followed in her footsteps, even her youngest despite his untimely death. Yet, her oldest and his family have experienced this generational agreement (blessings) and are in a thriving fellowship where they minister also.

When someone in the family agrees to allow this generational content, it causes a ripple effect. However, someone in the family can also come into agreement with darkness. They likely did not know what they were doing or that their agreement would affect their future generations.

Generational Stronghold

A generational stronghold can be pressures within you that are being held at bay, and are not truly gone and/or issues which come back regularly.

For instance, when someone who has dealt with depression and/or drug addiction for many years gets born again; they are fine for a while, but then something happens where they feel they can't cope. Therefore, they revert back to their "old ways" of dealing with these pressures by obtaining the drugs and taking a hit of whatever they had. Then when that wears off- the guilt sets in and they fall on their knees to God and ask for His forgiveness. Until the next incident happens that throws them back into those pressures and feeling like the only way they can cope is to give in to the stronghold. In a case like this, deliverance is needed. Same with alcohol addiction.

Ripples are less likely at this level because multiple family members had to have personally come into agreement with the generational content. You or the person affected by generational strongholds will need to repent and do some inner healing work to release the stronghold within.

Science Confirms Biblical Truths

While writing this book, the Holy Spirit brought this article by Soul Refiner Blogger Jeremy Wiles to my attention: "Science Confirms Bible on Generational Curses." This read revealed a Biblical truth through science and helped confirm why some patterns in your family seem to recur in your life. The church has long believed [generational curses] were purely spiritual. However, according to new brain research, this biblical principle is far more scientific than we realize.

What is Epigenetics?

Even though we can trace generational curses back to Exodus 20:5, pioneering studies in epigenetics reveal that our life experiences and choices change us, including our brains, down to the DNA level. These changes can be passed onto our children and further down the hereditary line. A study called epigenetics gives insight into how our diets, work environment, and even one-off traumatic events (including slavery, war, terrorist attacks, pandemics, etc.) can change the genetic legacy we pass onto our children and grandchildren.

Epigenetics is information that sits above the genome, which controls the programming of DNA, instructing different cells how to express themselves. In an interview from the Conquer Series, a new men's video-based teaching series, neuropsychologist Dr. Jess Montgomery explains, *"Sensations we put into the brain will use the DNA to change how the cell responds. And those genes are turned 'off' or 'on' based on that response. While the DNA does not change, the expression does."*

Therefore, our environment affects our gene expressions and how we function and behave. This quiet scientific revolution could be a paradigm shift for evolutionary biology, as it refutes Darwin's central premise. Neuropsychologist Dr. Tim Jennings said, *"Which is more scientifically accurate – the Bible or Charles Darwin? Well guess what? It is the Bible. Darwin hypothesized that it was mutation over millions of years that caused finches to have different beaks. Science has actually now proved; it is epigenetic modification. This is big because science is now confirming scripture."*

Epigenetics reveals that not only do we pass along the DNA sequence to our children, but we also pass along the epigenetic instructions to them. In other words, information can be inherited and transmitted through generations. In an experiment on 'transgenerational epigenetic inheritance,' researchers at Emory University trained mice to fear a fruity odor by pairing it with a mild electric shock to the foot. Ten days later, the mice were allowed to mate. Incredibly, their pups feared the odor even without encountering the smell. But even more fascinating is that the offspring of those pups – the grandchildren – were born with the same specific memory. We see the mice study apply to humans. One example was the attacks of 9/11. Among the thousands of people directly exposed to the attack were 1,700 pregnant women. Some of these women developed symptoms of post-traumatic stress disorder (PTSD). Their children reacted with elevated levels of fear and stress around loud noises, unfamiliar people, or new foods. It seems the infants inherited the nightmare their mothers experienced that day.

Sins of The Father

It is cathartic when you can literally put the concept of generational curses under the microscope. Suddenly, your habits and experiences have far more significant social implications because you no longer live life just for yourself but for your descendants, too. As Jennings points out, *"The choices we make – the foods that we eat, the things that we watch – can affect how the DNA is expressed. When we have kids, we pass on the sequence to them. So, if we become addicted to stuff, we can pass along to our children gene instructions that make them more vulnerable to addictions."* From food addictions like coffee and sugar to tobacco, drugs, and alcohol, even pornography is an addiction that can be passed down through our generation to our kids.

Take pornography addiction, for instance, since it is the fastest-growing epidemic in today's church. According to a recent study, 65% of Christian men and 15% of Christian women are addicted to porn. Most likely, they are unaware of the hereditary ramifications of viewing porn. "It doesn't happen generally with one exposure to pornography. It's the repetitive exposure to pornography that will cause this type of gene expression change to happen," explains Jennings.

Dr. Ted Roberts, a sex addiction therapist and the host of the Conquer Series, said, "Probably the most devastating consequence is that God guarantees you – His Word is clear: 'the curse will be visited to the third and fourth generation.' If you are in sexual bondage or you are struggling with that and do not deal with it, it will be passed on to your kids."

Breaking the Curse

The good news is that even if epigenetic modifications are passed onto your offspring, they are reversible. In other words, it is possible to break the curse. *"You can go either way. We can pass along both positive things in our life and or negative, depending on the choices we make in life,"* said Jennings.

But here is the million-dollar question: If a Christian is set free from his past after being born-again, why are there so many believers who still see the effects of generational curses in their lives? Could it be because so many of us still live under the law? The law tells us that God's blessings are conditional, depending on how good we are, which is based on our works. In contrast, grace tells us that Christ took the curse upon himself on the Cross: Christ has redeemed us from the curse of the law, having become a curse for us.

Galatians 3:13 reads, *"...for it is written, 'Cursed is everyone who hangs on a tree."*

The law condemns us, but grace gives us the gift of non-condemnation. Once we are gripped by grace, we can indeed have the mind of Christ, which transforms our behavior and infuses all our relationships. Suddenly, we are empowered to break the curses, knowing that the blood of Christ covers us. This transformation is physically revealed in the genetic changes in our bodies but also in the legacy we will be leaving behind.

Understanding epigenetics means we no longer have to be victims of predetermined genetic codes. Spiritually speaking – we do not have to live under the curse and subject our children to it. Because of the Cross, the generational curses in our family can be broken. Science is merely discovering these powerful biblical truths. Being under grace, we can choose to turn the tide of generational curses into blessings. As marriage counselor, Dr. Doug Weiss said, *"Don't think of it as a battle that you're just fighting for yourself. You are fighting for the very lineage that God gave you. And if you break this curse, then your sons and your daughters have a better shot, and your grandchildren have a better shot."* The time is now to destroy every root of generational curses in our families in Jesus' Mighty Name!

Praying through Generational Healing:

Here are 7 steps listed below to help with generational healing when combined with prayer and believing the scriptures.

1. Identify the generational sin, curse, or negative pattern

2. Forgive whoever let it into the family line (you do not have to know who it was to forgive)

3. Repent for any personal participation in the sin

4. Repent on behalf of your family line

5. Release any emotions tied to the generational content, handing them over to Jesus

6. Remove the generational content, all its works and effects, by asking Jesus to clean it off your family tree. Ask that it be blocked from affecting any future generations.

7. Receive a blessing in place of cursing. Ask Jesus to restore anything lost or stolen by this generational content. Ask that a generational blessing would take its place. Scripture also tells us that generational blessing affects the family up to 1,000 generations later. (Exodus 20:6)

Prayer for Release from Generational Rejection

Proclaim the following prayer aloud:

Almighty and everlasting God, whose will it is to restore all things in your well-beloved Son, the King of kings and the Lord of lords, I thank you for all of those in previous generations who passed down to me peace, love, and an opportunity to know you and your Son, Jesus Christ.

I invite You into all of the sinful and hurting places of the past generations of my family lines, to those who may have suffered rejection, self-rejection, fear of rejection, self-condemnation, lack of self-worth, fear of failure, loneliness, perceived rejection, or feelings of abandonment. Please send the light and blood of Jesus (shed for the forgiveness of sins) back into all the pain-filled and empty places in the hearts of my family and heal them in Jesus' Holy Name.

Those in past generations have sinned against me and hurt me by participating in behaviors, activities, and acts that have caused rejection and all of the related feelings previously mentioned and associated with this unholy condition. Let me, O Lord, stand in their stead and plead repentance for them before your heavenly throne. Forgive them, Lord, because, in many cases, they did not know what they were doing. Please forgive them and break the hold these involvements have had on me. Release those here, O Lord, from the sins of their forefathers and mothers, even to the third or fourth generation, as written in your Holy Scriptures (Ex. 20:5).

Cover me with your blood, spilled at Calvary. I send your love and forgiveness back to those who hurt me or who hurt other members of my family line. I ask you to forgive them and to bring them into wholeness and newness of life in you. Please take all of the hurts and pain away that I have experienced from critical words spoken to me that have caused me to feel unloved and unwanted. Forgive those in my family who have been critical of my appearance and my mental or physical abilities, as well as of others.

I ask you to forgive me for any way I may have given in to the tendency to sin in the same way as my forebearers. Forgive and restore me to life and health as only you can.

In Jesus' Name, I pray. Amen.

Inner Healing Prayer Against Rejection
Proclaim the following prayer aloud:

Lord Jesus Christ, I believe that you are the Son of God and the only way to God the Father. You died on the cross for my sins, and you rose again from the dead.

I repent of all my sins and forgive everyone as if God would forgive me. I forgive all those who have rejected me, hurt me, and failed to show me love, Lord, and I trust you also to forgive me and them.

I believe Lord, that you do accept me. Right now, I acknowledge that I am accepted because of what you did for me on the cross. I am highly favored. I am the object of your special care. You really love me. You want me. Your Father is my Father. Heaven is my eternal home. I am a member of the family of God, the best family in the universe. Thank you! Thank You, Lord!

One more thing, Lord: I accept myself the way you made me. I am your workmanship, and I thank you for what you have created. I believe that you have begun a good work in me and that you will carry it on to completion until my life ends (Phil. 1:6, 1 Thess. 5:24).

Lord, so that your forgiveness can be fully effective in me, I now forgive myself for doing all the things I have brought before you in prayer, and I release myself from previous feelings of guilt and from constantly going back into the past when I have already asked for your forgiveness.

I break any bondage, condemning myself and judging myself as unacceptable to you and others. Release me from these self-destructive thoughts and behaviors in the precious name of Jesus. And now, Lord, I bind the spirits of rejection, self-rejection, perceived rejection, and fear of rejection in the blessed name of Jesus Christ. I break the adversary's power over me and command him to leave, in Jesus' name. I renounce any territory that was given to him, and I joyfully give it back to God.
I proclaim my release from any dark and evil spirits that have taken advantage of the past woundedness in my life. I release my spirit to rejoice in the Lord. In Jesus' name, I pray. Amen.

Church Hurt

*"All this is from God, who reconciled us to himself through Christ and gave us the ministry of reconciliation: **19** that God was reconciling the world to himself in Christ, not counting people's sins against them. And he has committed to us the message of reconciliation."*

2 Corinthians 5:18-19

God has given us the "ministry of reconciliation," but what does reconciliation look like when the one who's hurt you is a leader in your church? Church hurt and spiritual abuse are unfortunately common in today's churches. At times, unloving shepherds who lack compassion mistreat the sheep in their care. Sometimes, hurt is unintentional and caused by poor communication or insensitivity. At other times, there is explicit abuse, manipulation, or toxic religion.

The emotional fallout from rejection or mistreatment by a pastor or other shepherd serving in Jesus' name requires loving, tender empathy and guided healing. After a relationship breach, reconciliation requires that you move toward the other with God's love. Reconciliation is only possible as we receive and are compelled by Christ's love (2 Cor 5:14). Even if you were hurt by a parent, pastor, or other leader who should have been the one to make the first move, regardless, the ball is in your court to be the one to move toward the other with God's love and forgiveness.

Often, reconciliation requires significant work in setting boundaries, processing through forgiveness, and speaking the truth in love. There are other times when it's unsafe for you to reconcile with a leader who harmed you. If you've been abused, reconciliation is not wise, at least for the time being. You must then set healthy boundaries, seek emotional healing from a spiritual director or other support person, and engage in a forgiveness process. Regardless of which approach the Lord leads us in, we can follow Jesus' teaching, "Love one another… Love one another…" (John 13:34-35, 15:12), which He modeled by loving the religious leaders who crucified him.

Have you ever been bullied? Maybe it wasn't intentional, but have you ever felt abused? I have. And so have many of the people we help; even Jesus was bullied and abused, yet repair is possible! There are pastors who have no spiritual covering and have had several extra marital affairs with women in their church. He controls some of the females in his congregation with fear. He reprimands them when they miss a service or a Bible study and requires them to ask his permission to do certain things. He is not repentant at all but operates in a spirit of pride. These women need to run for the hills and get out of this man's grip. Say this quick little prayer if you've ever been bullied or abused by a leader or pastor at the church:

"Jesus, you are our Good Shepherd. Shepherd our hearts with your love and heal the hurt that may still wound your beloved sheep. In Jesus Name, I pray. Amen."

Church Hurt is Soul-Crushing

One of the problems that irks me the most is when a church leader in a position of authority misrepresents or distorts someone's view of God by acting abusively. Church hurt can cut you to the core. Much like our parents, we see church leaders as having authority. We look to them to lead us and shepherd us well. We trust them with our hearts and with our areas of vulnerability. When the people we trust manipulate, shame, reject, or use others for selfish gain, the effects are harrowing and confusing. It hits us where we are most tender, causing us to question God and our sense of worth. In some cases, the pain can cause one to wonder,

- If the church can deeply hurt me, what does that say about God?
- Who is God anyway?
- Can God be trusted after all?

I have been hurt by church leadership, and to be honest, a few times, all I had to do was sit back and watch everything implode, but the other times, it hurt me to my very core. I questioned, "How could they do this to me?" "What did I do to deserve this?" In addition, church hurt can damage how you think about yourself. Rejection can try to rear its ugly head again but you have the authority to stop it! Rationally, you might know the pain is not your fault. But parts of you can still wonder if you did something wrong. Toxic shame enters your mind, and you might start wondering, "If that church represents God, then how could they be wrong? What if I am the problem? What if I deserved what I got?"

Let's be honest. The process of healing from church hurt is not easy. It can be hard to face the pain. It can be hard to disentangle the God who loves you from the misrepresentation of God by an unhealthy leader. Understandably, many people get angry and stay bitter. Others leave the church altogether, but there is another way through. If you are struggling with the pain of church hurt or if a church misrepresented God to you through toxic, abusive actions or words, please know you are not alone. You are still in the center of God's love *and* justice because God hates church hurt, too!

Matthew 18:6 confirms, *"But if you give them a hard time, bullying or taking advantage of their simple trust, you will soon wish you had not. You would be better off dropped in the middle of the lake with a millstone around your neck. Doom to the world for giving these God-believing children a hard time! Hard times are inevitable, but you do not have to make it worse- and it is doomsday to you if you do."*

4 Steps to Heal from Church Hurt

1. Define Church Hurt as Abuse

Church leaders hold power; yes, that is true, but great power includes great responsibility. If someone misuses their power, the result is defined as "abuse," which means to act in a manner to cause "bad effect or for a bad purpose; misuse" (Oxford Languages Dictionary). Church hurt stems from experiencing someone else abusing their power.

A church has the power to gather, encourage, and heal God's beloved people. On the positive side, the church can help you:

- Encourage yourself and others (1 Thessalonians 5:11; Hebrews 10:25)

- Give thanks and marvel at God's wonders (Colossians 3:16)
- Grow in humble, honest self-awareness (James 4:8
- Pray with other people (Acts 2:42)
- Grow in wisdom and knowledge of God (Ephesians 3:10)
- Care for those who are most vulnerable (James 1:27)

In contrast, when a church leader abuses their power, it has the opposite effect, such as causing:

- Discouragement and disappointment in yourself and others
- Feelings of anger, confusion, and bitterness toward God
- Toxic movement toward rigid self-denial and self-hatred
- Bypassing or denial of pain and emotions (vs. bringing them to God honestly)
- False ideas about God (vs. the God Jesus embodied)
- Further wounds on the most vulnerable

To heal, you must be able to identify church hurt as abuse; therefore, here are some examples below:

- He attacked the young girl that God made. *That was an abuse of church power.*
- She taught me I was not worthy of God's love. *That was an abuse of church power.*
- They told my secrets to others and called it prayer. *That was an abuse of church power.*
- He told me that my abusive husband's behavior was my fault. *That was an abuse of church power.*
- She said my depression was evidence that I lacked faith. *That was an abuse of church power.*

Recognizing church hurt helps not to harbor resentment. The initial healing process hinges upon you naming the sinful behavior that occurred. You may have gone through these in every church you attended, served, and were a member of. Each time you experienced hurt, that root grew deeper and wider. Each time you experienced hurt, you found yourself becoming more bitter, more frustrated, angrier, and questioning God. Have you made this comment, "Here we go around that mountain again"? It's the same hurt, different church, huh?

2. Separate the Church Hurt from God's Character

Aspects of God's character are evident throughout the Bible; therefore, separating the church hurt from who God is is essential. If you feel broken or beaten down by a church community, step back momentarily and remind yourself who God is apart from the hurtful actions. And more than that, remind yourself who YOU are in Christ- and remember your identity as a child of God for instance:

- God loves justice, mercy, and humility. (Micah 6:8)
- God is for the poor in spirit, the grief-stricken, the humble, the broken-hearted, and the peacemakers (Matthew 5:1-12)
- God stands against the proud and for the humble (James 4:6)
- God is love (1 John 4:7)
- God's presence shows up as love, joy, peace, patience, kindness, goodness, faithfulness, gentleness, and self-control (Galatians 5:22-23)

Look at the life of Jesus and notice how he interacted with various types of people. He was clear about his stance toward individuals in these three categories:

> **Abusers of Power:**

Jesus gave his harshest words to religious leaders who judged, criticized, oppressed, and left people out. These folks created cliques and always attempted to maintain their power through abuse. If you're not convinced that Jesus was harsh with unhealthy religious leaders, read these passages: *Matthew 23, Mark 9:42, Luke 11:43-44.*

> ## The Sufferers:

Jesus drew close to hurting, wounded, sick, and suffering people. He did not blame them for their suffering or marginalize them. Instead, he encouraged, helped, and treated them with respect. Read some of the life-giving stories of how Jesus interacted with suffering in these passages: *Luke 17:12–16, John 9:6–7.*

> ## The Marginalized:

Jesus also showed a soft spot for those on the outs, such as "sinners," rebels, and the people who others tended to despise. For example, do you remember the woman who got caught in adultery? Jesus purposefully intervened to protect her. In another story, Jesus first revealed his true identity to a woman from Samaria, a place equivalent to "the wrong side of the tracks," and she'd been divorced four times. Read more stories of Jesus siding with marginalized individuals in these passages: *Mark 2:15–16, Luke 7:36–39, John 4:25, 26.*

You will have a powerful ally as you identify God's desire to help hurting people. God is on the side of those who have suffered, not on the side of those who abuse their power.

3. Recover Your Power

If you have experienced church hurt, it can make you feel helpless and alone, but to reclaim your power, you must set boundaries with those responsible for the pain. Then, heal from the agony inside your soul. But, to heal, you will need the help of safe people. Here are some ways to start that process:

> ## Prioritize your emotional recovery first.

It is not your job to empathize with those in power who hurt you. There might be a time for forgiveness or reconciliation down the road. But it is far more critical that you separate yourself from the harm and restore the parts of yourself that were wounded.

> ## Seek support outside of the church.

If your church culture is toxic, seeking a healthy perspective from someone outside that environment is crucial. For instance, contact a counselor or trusted adviser who can help you stay clear and grounded as you deal with the church hurt and find your way to solid ground.

> ➤ **Wait to communicate until you have a strong support network.**

Once you are clear about the nature of your church hurt, you might try communicating boundaries with the leaders of a church community, but please do NOT take this step alone. I have watched several episodes of the TV series Greenleaf on OWN Network, and this show is a good picture of abusive power in a church- and some of us know all too well this is precisely how some churches operate. I have seen and experienced it- and nobody who faced that giant head-on survived.

It is wise to enlist help to ensure that you do not get pulled back up into a web of toxicity and experience more harm. Follow what Matthew 18:15 says,

"If another believer sins against you, go privately and point out the offense. If the other person listens and confesses it, you have won that person back."

If you decide to confront a hurtful leader, ensure you have support. Then, pay close attention to the response. You will quickly learn if that person is messy but loving or toxic, and if that is the case, then it is probably time to find a new church community. Most of the church communities I encountered were toxic- they had built their empires and only wanted certain people in their "inner circle." If you were not a fit, you were treated like an outsider in the worst ways.

4. Reclaim Your Spiritual Practices

As you reclaim your power, you can also reclaim some spiritual practices. But, just like any physical wound, certain situations may rekindle more pain. With emotional pain, there may be specific words and practices that seem normal to everyone else, such as prayer or listening to a sermon. Still, they bring up uncomfortable and painful feelings within you. Those practices got twisted due a leader's abusive actions. Again, that seed of bitterness grows, and that root goes deeper.

For example, if someone betrayed your trust while claiming to "pray" for you, their actions could make the idea of prayer feel uncomfortable.

Likewise, specific Bible verses may have been used to manipulate you, which might bring up painful feelings when you hear those passages again. In situations like those, notice your feelings and react gently. It doesn't mean that you don't love God. It is quite the opposite! God is developing essential skills, such as discernment, to help you discern when to trust versus when to sound the danger alarm. You are learning to discover Jesus apart from the leaders who misrepresented Him. As long as you keep a spirit of haughtiness from growing in your heart, you will continue to grow and learn. But always remember Proverbs 16:18: pride comes before the fall.

"Pride goes before destruction, and a haughty spirit before a fall."

Remember who Jesus is, and keep your eyes on Him because man's human nature will always hurt you...always. Turn the negative into a positive by redefining old harmful words into new terms. For example, think of "prayer" as just a loving way to talk with God. You could even keep your eyes open and look at something beautiful or comforting that reminds you of God's love. Talk to God aloud, listen to soothing music, walk with a friend, or write in a journal. The Bible tells us that when several people are gathered in meaningful, honest connection, God is there with them.

Matthew 18:20, *"For where two or three are gathered together in my name, there am I in the midst of them."*

Above all, God is Against "Church Hurt."

The church is supposed to be a refuge, a safe haven- not a place of toxicity and abuse. God desires to meet you in tender places and provide healing. He does not force, control, or manipulate. Once you begin your healing process by defining church hurt as abuse, separate the hurtful behavior from God's character, recover your power, and reclaim your spiritual practices, God wants to restore the goodness in your life that an abusive leader took away. You are never alone in the miraculous power of God's love. Recall any repressed memories—as difficult as they may be. God is ready to heal those "church-hurt memories." Your loving Heavenly Father does not want you "going around that mountain again and again."

**Disclaimer: This chapter does not say that every time you have a misunderstanding, an offense, or a falling out with a church leader, it is an abuse of power. We live in a fallen world, and there will always be times when we get offended or upset with leadership because that is the devil's strategy. We must go to God with that offense or frustration and not hold it inside or gossip to anyone else about the situation. They are, after all, our leaders and humans; therefore, it is our job to pray for them. Church hurt is *only* when church leaders overstep their boundaries, and it becomes the *abuse* that we then see this chapter come to life.

PTSD

Post-Traumatic Stress Disorder is Characterized by:

1) Direct experience of an event that involves actual or threatened death or serious injury. PTSD includes learning about such a thing happening to someone close to them. PTSD includes betrayal of trust, violation of the body zone, and other things. The person feels helpless and deeply threatened at a survival level. Something happened that they did not have control over and overwhelmed their conscious & emotional resources.

2) There is a lack of social support to stop and safely deal with the memories through grief work. There is a lack of other good memories to fall back on. Children have none. Trauma is repressed or suppressed to the subconscious instead. The empowered subconscious is neither Christian nor moral. It is vulnerable to demonic infestation, but it can defend itself.

3) The subconscious expresses it by:

    a. Re-experiencing the trauma through dreams, body sensations, and waking thoughts.

    b. Panicked, enraged, or shut down by indirect reminders (paranoia).

    c. Re-enacting the trauma unconsciously in metaphor or directly by using someone else in one of the roles.

    d. Emotional numbing to other life experiences and relationships causes an inability to relax and engage in recreation, leading to the use of drugs and manic behavior to numb the trauma.

e. Avoiding reminders in their environment (xenophobia).

f. Regressive behaviors to an age before major trauma or resorting to drugs as an attempted escape.

g. Forgiveness by the conscious mind does not stop the above. The subconscious can lead to bitterness and unforgiveness.

4) Symptoms of autonomic instability, sleeplessness, depression, and cognitive difficulties (such as poor concentration).

5) Traumas are more apt to become corporate PTSD in sick families where bad times are endemic (of a disease or condition regularly found among particular people or in a specific area) and hidden as a habit. No support is offered for recovery. Everyone acts out part of the PTSD. This kind of trauma is called "codependence."

If there were severe physical, sexual, psychological, or religious abuse suffered at an early age, the resulting Multiple Personality Disorder (MPD) or Dissociative Identity Disorder (DID) personality segments would hold the memory of that abuse. If they are led to Christ and fused without the memories they hold brought to light and healed in the traumatized person, that person will face unnecessary future difficulties in life, perhaps never fully healed.

Jesus Comes to Heal When We Ask.

The essential points of praying over PTSD are this:

1. You need to read the above characterization of PTSD.

2. Close your eyes and remember one of the situations this evoked.

3. Pray aloud: *"I ask the Lord Jesus to speak Truth into this memory."*

4. Wait a minute or two in silence. You may suddenly become elated, or you might feel like nothing happened. If you did not feel anything, ask if the presenting problem (shame, rejection, defensiveness, and depression) is still there and ask Jesus what to do with it.

5. This process can also be repeated and multiplied for other traumas.

Have you experienced an event or events in your life that were so traumatic that you were outside the realm of everyday experience? If so, trauma may have shaped your mind and body toward anxiety, just as it can shape the mind and body toward depression. If this resonates with you, look at the lists below:

Mind Symptoms of PTSD

- Experienced painful emotional or physical trauma in their family growing up.

- Suffered emotional or physical trauma in one or more relationships.

- There has been an event in their life in which they have been threatened with such severe physical or emotional harm that it would be out of the range of what we consider average life experience.

- Some examples might be living through war, witnessing an accident with loss of life or limb, experiencing rape or incest, or seeing children suffer abuse.

- Whatever the trauma they have experienced, they tend to have "repeat performances" of this painful pattern in one relationship after another, one job after another, and so on. The painful pattern, like the movie Groundhog Day, seems to replay repeatedly in their life.

- Thought patterns of terror, fright, panic, and edginess.

- Feeling that they might be hurt or harmed or that someone might reject or criticize them.

- Believe they will not get the help they need.

- Feeling incompetent to change the situation.

- Feel like they are going crazy.

PTSD is real, and it is NO laughing matter. And I believe it can only be genuinely dealt with on a spiritual basis.

Body Symptoms of PTSD

In addition to the symptoms in the previous section, you may have these:

- Trembling and shaking
- Hot flashes and cold chills
- Numbness and tingling
- Nausea or a sick feeling in your stomach
- Pressure in your chest
- A pounding heart
- Cold sweats
- Shortness of breath
- A lump in your throat
- Dizziness and vertigo
- Feeling like you are "out of your body"
- Feeling like you are dying

I had a family member take his own life due to the struggles he had from more than 50 years of PTSD. He lost his family, including his children. They couldn't reach him. He went through counseling, became a Christian, went through more counseling, and still struggled. His last words were, "I can't live with my demons anymore". I've experienced this stronghold and I know PTSD is real. It is important that we educate ourselves We must learn how to bring healing to those hurting from it. Take some intentional time to pray and spiritually war against the darlness of PTSD and trust that by His stripes you are healed

Prayer for PTSD

Father, I take authority over anything that wants to insert itself, distract, disturb, interfere, or otherwise mess with the administration of this prayer. I kick to the curb anything that will not bow its knee to the name of the Lord Jesus Christ; anything that you, Father God, have not placed there, I give you no place here or there in Jesus' name. I take authority over this time, this space, this place, this dimension in the name of the Lord Jesus Christ. Father, please disconnect them from the effects of assignments of generationally transferred trauma. Suppose there is any portion of them that has been removed is stuck, imprisoned, or held captive in any other time, space, place, or dimension as a result of the trauma experienced. In that case, I ask that you immediately send your angels to rescue them, release them, and cause those portions of them to be recovered from wherever it has been, and I ask that you restore and cleanse them of any defilement of any place it has been.

In Jesus' name, I command their body to release all the long- and short-term effects of trauma, everything that it has held onto down to the cellular level, from all the accidents, injuries, medical procedures, surgeries, invasive medical procedures, broken bones, cuts, hearing and deafness issues, vision, and eye impairments. I also command their bodies to release all the effects of trauma concerning rejection, abandonment, death, deep depression, divorce, loss of dreams, hopes, and aspirations. Every time that they were robbed and stolen from, yelled or screamed at, pushed, shoved, beaten, held captive, shot, stabbed, subjected to explosive blasts, tortured and tormented, the emotional, spiritual and physical effects of childhood accidents and injuries, operations, invasive medical procedures, childhood fears, loss of a key loved one by death, witnessing the death, destruction, wounding, or dismemberment of a fellow soldier, divorce, or abandonment, rape, abuse (physical, mental, emotional, or sexual), frequent moves, car accidents, major illnesses, broken bones, attempted suicide, deep depressions, near-death experiences, catastrophic events that occurred as part of the war and military action, hurricanes and earthquakes, civilian casualties related to war and combat experiences, the effects of difficult childbirths, miscarriages, or abortions. I ask you, Holy Spirit, to restore to life the broken, dead, and dormant places, the places that have been wounded and given up on, that have been set aside, ignored, rejected, shut down, and abandoned. I call for a restoration and redemptive work within them at the deepest levels. And Father, would you give them a tangible sense that they are not alone, a concrete knowing that you are with them through this?

Announce and confess your freedom.

I announce and confess that I am free today. In Jesus' Name, I pray. Amen

Anxiety and Depression

***DISCLAIMER: I am NOT a doctor, nor do I claim to be or have any medical training or knowledge in the area of anxiety—but what I can and will tell you is what the Word of God says can heal your soul wounds, your body, and your mind.

Anxiety is a tremendous stronghold in our world today. Most people who follow Jesus turn to Him in their time of need, i.e., praying for God to supply every need, healing relationships, and physical healing. In the same way, when you suffer times of anxiety, most people instinctively turn to Jesus. For those following Christ, it just makes sense to turn to Him for help dealing with anxiety. But we do not just want you to "turn" to Him for help with the anxiety- we want you to go beyond and take the next step—and the next step. Answers to anxiety are available in the Word- but for so many, that doesn't seem to bring much relief. You can read "Do not be afraid," yet still be anxious. We want to deal with the roots of anxious feelings, which usually lie in past trauma. We also want to build up your spiritual immunity system so that you can be healed from anxiety and the trauma of it. We want to deal with the fruit, get to the root, and become aligned with what God's Word says about us.

Fear, anxiety, and worry plague and torment both believers and unbelievers alike. Since the fall of man, the enemy has made it seem natural for us to worry, to fret, to fear something in our past, present, and future because that is his plan to deceive us. Worry may seem to be normal to us, and that is because the enemy has lied to us; however, worrying is also sinful. That's because most elevated emotions, such as fear, anxiety, and worry, are a failure to trust God and His goodness or to believe what He told us.

Psalm 55:22 NIV, *Cast your cares on the Lord, and he will sustain you; he will never let the righteous be shaken.*

Jesus knows that worry is a powerful weapon the enemy uses against us. This battlefield against fear, anxiety, and worry is done in our minds. However, in Matthew 6:25-34 Jesus promised us that we could walk in freedom just like He did here on Earth.

Even David, close to God's heart, could not keep himself from fear, anxiety, and worry. He dealt with the fear of death because of Saul and his son Absalom. You can read from many of his Psalms that he cried for the Lord to help him as the enemies tried to pull him down. But David was evident and had a deep understanding within his heart that God is his rock, protector, and refugee in times of distress:

The Lord is my rock, my fortress and my deliverer; my God is my rock, in whom I take refuge, my shield and the horn of my salvation, my stronghold.
Psalm 18:2 (NIV)

Fear, Anxiety, and Worry were perhaps as much a common disorder in biblical times as it is today, and the causes of and reasons for it are about the same as those of today. The apostle Paul gave us instructions on how to deal with worry.

In Philippians 4:6 (TPT), *"Be saturated in prayer throughout each day, offering your faith-filled requests before God with overflowing gratitude."*

Phillippians 4:8 (CJB), *"...focus our thoughts on what is true, noble, righteous, pure, lovable or admirable, on some virtue or on something praiseworthy".*

Isaiah 43:1 (NIV), *"Don't fear, for I have redeemed you; I have called you by name; you are Mine."*

God Commands Us Not to Fear or Worry.

When you let fear in, you are not using your faith and trusting in the Lord. I read an article about an inner healing and deliverance ministry session where the prayer minister worked with a woman suffering in her life. She said, *"Fear and anxiety had such a strong gripping hand on my life."* She had financial debt problems due to her business loss and faced anxiety for many years without being able to come out of it. It wasn't until she came to know Jesus Christ as Lord that things started to change for her. Once they found the root of the dissociative, wounded parts of the soul for her anxiety, they began the healing process for Jesus to come and take the pain away permanently."

Tim Tomlinson Ministries

The Lord is close to the brokenhearted and saves those who are crushed in spirit.

Psalm 34:18 (NIV)

The truth is Satan is attacking your mind, and does so because of your soul wounds. Soul/heart wounds are caused by hurt and trauma at any age in your life, and they can be from friends, family, and even enemies that you may come in contact with. Trauma is usually associated with accidents, physical abuse, verbal abuse, sexual abuse, physical pain, or any emotional pain that you can't handle or cope with at that moment. Since past hurts and soul wounds haven't been healed by Jesus, they open the doorway, which causes the enemy to torment us. (Matthew 18:23-35)

Remember, it is the unbelieving part of a believer's heart that has not accepted the new life in Christ and the healing.

If not healed, those past hurts will start showing up in your life because a portion of your heart is still broken. You can't fix it yourself as much as you want, so you must seek Godly people specializing in inner healing and deliverance. Be careful seeking out ministry from a source that has yet to be recognized and set forth by leadership. There are always people running around wanting to pray for you and cast devils out of you, yet the Bible says to *know* them that labor among you. Only let people lay their hands on you if you know the ministry, especially any novices because this is the easiest way to transfer wrong spirits this way.

1 Thessalonians 5:12, *"And we urge you, brethren, to recognize those who labor among you, and are over you in the Lord and admonish you."*

The enemy torments you through these past soul wounds, and it can affect you in your body through sickness, pain, and undiagnosed medical conditions. It also affects your soul and mind by feelings of hopelessness that bring with it elevated emotions such as fear, anxiety, anger, rejection, abandonment, or despair. Your soul wounds can also affect your family, job, and friends.

"The thief comes only to steal and kill and destroy; I have come that they may have life, and have it to the full." John 10:10 (NIV)

Satan is a thief and very sneaky; he is responsible more often than we think. He is the cause of your torrent of fear, anxiety, worry, pain, etc. Inner healing is just one of the many reasons Christ died on the cross (Ephesians 1:7). God wants to heal our deepest hurts, and that's where inner healing comes in, as you learned in Chapter 1 of this text.

Psalm 147:3 NIV, "He heals the brokenhearted and binds up their wounds."

Some common anxiety signs and symptoms include:

- Feeling nervous, restless, or tense
- Having a sense of impending danger, panic, or doom
- Having an increased heart rate
- Breathing rapidly (hyperventilation)
- Sweating
- Trembling
- Feeling weak or tired
- Trouble concentrating or thinking about anything other than the present worry
- Having trouble sleeping
- Experiencing gastrointestinal (GI) problems
- Having difficulty controlling worry
- Having the urge to avoid things that trigger anxiety

According to Mayo Clinic, here are a few types of anxiety disorders:

- **Agoraphobia** (ag-uh-ruh-FOE-be-uh) is a type of anxiety disorder in which you fear and often avoid places or situations that might cause you to panic and make you feel trapped, helpless, or embarrassed.

• **Anxiety disorder due to a medical condition** includes symptoms of intense anxiety or panic that are directly caused by a physical health problem.

• **Generalized anxiety disorder** includes persistent and excessive anxiety and worry about activities or events — even ordinary, routine issues. It often occurs along with other anxiety disorders or depression.

• **Panic disorder** involves repeated episodes of sudden feelings of intense anxiety and fear or terror that reach a peak within minutes (panic attacks). You may have feelings of impending doom, shortness of breath, chest pain, or a rapid, fluttering, or pounding heart (heart palpitations). These panic attacks may lead to worrying about them happening again or avoiding situations in which they've occurred.

• **Separation anxiety disorder** is a childhood disorder characterized by anxiety that's excessive for the child's developmental level and related to separation from parents or others who have parental roles.

• **Social anxiety disorder (social phobia)** involves high levels of anxiety, fear, and avoidance of social situations due to feelings of embarrassment, self-consciousness, and concern about being judged or viewed negatively by others.

• **Specific phobias** are characterized by major anxiety when you're exposed to a specific object or situation and a desire to avoid it. Phobias provoke panic attacks in some people.

• **Substance-induced anxiety disorder** is characterized by symptoms of intense anxiety or panic that are a direct result of misusing drugs, taking medications, being exposed to a toxic substance, alcohol, or withdrawal from drugs.

• **Other specified anxiety disorders and unspecified anxiety disorders** are terms for anxiety or phobias that don't meet the exact criteria for any other anxiety disorders but are significant enough to be distressing and disruptive.

One way that will help you get to the root of your anxiety is two-way journaling, which is going to play a big part in your healing. You can do this by setting aside some quiet time each day and doing 2-way journaling, asking Holy Spirit to reveal to you the roots and causes of any anxiety. *Write them in your journal, then say this prayer:*

<u>Prayer for Anxiety</u>

Father God, I bless your name and declare that what the Bible teaches me about you is accurate. I declare that your very nature is love. Your love for me does not depend on my merit or favor. It is just who You are. Father, help me to feel secure in your love. I declare your love breaks down my fear and worries about my health, finances, relationships, and future. Father God, I ask you to put your loving, healing touch on my amygdala. Take the fearful emotions and negative memories that I may have stored in my brain and sanctify them. Any neurological patterns of fear and worry must now submit to your love! Father, remove the lies that have led me to believe that I will always have fear and anxiety and that I cannot change. I declare that I am not too old to change, and with your help, I will become a new person. I declare that your love will win the day! In Jesus' mighty name, I pray. Amen.

Ungodly Soul Ties

What is a Soul Tie?

The term "soul tie" is worldly and man-made and not mentioned in the Bible, however, the Bible does describe the idea when it talks about *"souls being knit together, becoming one flesh."*

1 Samuel 18:1, *"...the soul of Jonathan was knit with the soul of David, and Jonathan loved him as his own soul."*

1 Corinthians 6:16, *"Do you not know that he who unites himself with a prostitute is one with her in body? For it is said, "The two will become one flesh."*

A soul tie can serve many functions, but in its simplest form, it *ties two souls together in the spiritual realm.* Soul ties between married couples draw them together like magnets, while soul ties between fornicators can draw a beaten and abused woman to the man which in the *natural realm* she would hate and run from, but instead, she runs to him even though he doesn't love her and treats her like dirt.

In the demonic world, unholy soul ties can serve as bridges between two people to pass demonic garbage through. Relationships fill our lives and, in many ways, help define who we are. We are sons and daughters, brothers and sisters, husbands, wives, fathers, and mothers through relationships. In parallel with this, the Bible also teaches that we are spiritual beings, created in God's image - higher than animals. With God's Spirit breathed into us, we are primarily spirits, not just bodies and minds, as Western science teaches. There was a local man not too long ago who broke free from downright awful visitations from demons, all due to an ungodly soul tie he had with a witch when he had an affair. The man was a Christian, and the only thing that allowed this woman, aka witch, to send demonic torment his way was through the soul tie. Soul ties can do things such as allow one person to manipulate and control another person, and the other person is unaware of what is going on or knows what is going on, but for no real reason, allows it to continue.

How Soul Ties are Formed

Sexual relations: Godly soul ties are formed when a couple gets married.

> Ephesians 5:31, *"For this cause shall a man leave his father and mother, and shall be joined unto his wife, and they two shall be one flesh."*

The godly soul tie between a husband and wife God intended him to have is *unbreakable by man* (Mark 10:7-9). However, when a person has ungodly sexual relations with another person, an ungodly soul tie is then formed, as the scripture 1 Corinthians 6:16 describes. This soul tie fragments the soul and is *destructive*. People who have many past relationships find it difficult to 'bond' or be joined to anybody because their soul is fragmented through fornication(sexual intercourse between people not married to each other).

Close relationships: The relationship between King David and Jonathan, as mentioned in 1 Samuel 18:1, describes a good soul tie resulting from a good friendship. However, bad soul ties can form from bad relationships as well. For example, idolizing somebody can cause a bad soul tie. Also, you can create a soul tie with a rock group by becoming obsessed with their music, which explains the strong pull towards certain music that seems almost irresistible.

Vows, commitments, and agreements: Vows are known to bind the soul.

> Numbers 30:2 says, *"When a man makes a vow to the Lord or takes an oath to obligate himself by a pledge, he must not break his word but must do everything he said."*

Marriage consists of vows that bind the two people together.

> Ephesians 5:31, *"For this reason a man will leave his father and mother and be united to his wife, and the two will become one flesh."*

Therefore, I have little reason to overlook the concept of vows or commitments as a means to create a soul tie.

Male and Female Roles

Paul's teaching of women provokes arguments in many churches, but note that he *establishes an order only in marriage.* Paul does not intend to ban women from teaching men. He contradicts this idea in many other places in his affirmation of women's leadership in the church and community.

A valid translation of 1 Timothy 2:12 is, *"I do not permit a wife to teach (implying dominates or direct) or take authority over her husband; she must be quiet."*

The Greek word 'andros' means 'man' and 'warrior'. The Hebrew word "ruach" is a feminine word that means the 'Spirit, Wind, or Breath of Elohim'. The terms here are used as often in the context of marriage as they are for 'male' and 'female.' His instruction on the role of an elder also implies the relationship between 'teaching' and 'taking authority.'

1 Timothy 3:2, *"Now the overseer is to be above reproach, faithful to his wife, temperate, self-controlled, respectable, hospitable, able to teach."*

The world's obsession with power and control has distorted God's original design in the book of Genesis and reinforced it (or enforced it) based on the male's superior physical strength and enlarged ego. This male's superior mindset has fallen right into Satan's strategy - using the frustration of women to lead them into abusing their sexuality and using witchcraft to get their way.

Sex and Marriage

Along with the gift of sex, God has given us the precious gift of free will and choice. We are not to be driven by our desires or 'needs,' which is how the world sees sex - a primal urge that cannot and should not be denied.

Sex is permitted only within a life marriage covenant. Period! The choice is not open between sex in or out of marriage. The choice is between *sex in marriage* and *abstinence outside of marriage*. This decision is not an arbitrary law of God or the church because anything else will harm us and bring death and destruction into our relationships.

A sexual union is a spiritual union, but not necessarily a holy union. It can only be holy inside a marriage covenant. *The Holy Spirit will never participate in an immoral relationship* - something will always be missing. A spiritual covenant is established through sacrifice and death. In a marriage covenant, each lays down their life for the other, choosing to no longer live for self. This covenant creates a union, a life commitment, and ends only at the death of one of the parties. The world prefers to enter into a marriage contract, and contracts can be broken, but God ordained the marriage covenant to be binding.

The same marriage covenants are needed so children can grow up in a union blessed by God, which models the fundamental relationship between a man, a woman, and the Spirit of God. Life comes only from God; therefore; conception, birth, and growth right through to eventual release into teenage, adulthood, and marriage must occur in God's presence. With the parents modeling oneness, it's easier for a child to build a foundation for intimate relationships.

In Malachi 2:14-15, *"You ask, "Why?" It is because the Lord is the witness between you and the wife of your youth. You have been unfaithful to her, though she is your partner, the wife of your marriage covenant. Has not the one God made you? You belong to him in body and spirit. And what does the one God seek? Godly offspring. So be on your guard, and do not be unfaithful to the wife of your youth."*

Divorce

There are many scriptures in the Bible that discuss divorce. Read Deuteronomy 24:1-4, Matthew 5:31, 19:3-9, and 1 Corinthians 7:10-11 to see how God feels about divorce.

A well-known pastor, Rick Joyner, said, *"Discussion of divorce creates much heat within the church. I think it is best to remember that marriage is a covenant between two people and God. If necessary, God is able to release us from unfortunate or unwise covenants - but we must go to him about it, not just decide it between ourselves. I personally do not believe that divorce necessarily disqualifies us from leadership in the church, as this would even disqualify the Lord. We read in (Jeremiah 3:6-8), that God gave Israel a certificate of divorce - was it because He was not a good husband? Of course not. Even with a perfect husband Israel and Judah committed adultery with other gods. Each case must be looked at individually".*

To receive inner healing after a divorce, follow the prompts below to break free from this unhealthy soul tie:

- Confess any personal responsibility and receive God's forgiveness.
- Forgive those who caused the hurt or breakdown of the marriage.
- Confess breaking the marriage vows (either willingly or unwillingly).
- Ask the Lord to release you from the vow you made before God, witnesses, and your marriage partner.
- Release and bless your former partner.

Godly Sex and Godly Soul Ties

Genesis 2:18, *"The Lord God said, "It is not good for the man to be alone. I will make a helper suitable for him."*

There are many other scriptures to help us identify what godly soul ties are like: *Ephesians 5:31-33; 6:1-4; Phil 2:1-5; James 2:8*. We know that 'soul ties' are real bonds that hold us together, like superglue, in relationships. When we form a loving, healthy relationship with someone, we refer to it as a godly soul tie.

Some Examples of Godly Soul Ties:

- husband and wife
- parent and child

- siblings
- the wider family circle
- friends
- mentor and mentee
- brothers and sisters in the family of God

We have soul ties with our family as a result of birth, or we develop them with other people due to the decisions and choices we make through marriage, friendships, etc. Or we have ungodly soul ties forced upon us by abusive relationships like fear, rape, and cruelty, or we enter into them by becoming 'one flesh' with sexual partners, as declared in 1 Corinthians 6:16.

Remember, any sexual intercourse forms a soul tie. Vows to each other are made during a wedding ceremony - a covenant relationship before God. We vow to love each other and stay together until death parts us. This covenant is consummated through sexual intercourse - the man and woman become one flesh. A godly bond is created. God intended for it to be this way, and without sex, there is no marriage.

Authors John and Paula Sandford, in their book *Restoring the Christian Family*, describe the sexual union this way:

"Sexual blessedness, more than any other form of human encounter, depends upon our having become human beings. A human being is a person who has a loving, living personal spirit by which he empathizes with others and cherishes others more than himself. ...Sexual blessedness depends upon the capacity of our spirits to reach through our bodies to nurture, bless, enfold, enrich, and enrapture the heart and spirit of another.

A Godly soul tie is a Godly one-flesh bonding - a spiritual, emotional, mental, freewill, and physical tie. The blessing of God - who is part of this union - comes down on them and nurtures and encourages them. John and Paula have said that the Holy Spirit sings within the sexual union. Each of the couple now belongs to the other - they can never be separate again. Their body is no longer their own. Paul says do not withhold it from one another except for fasting and prayer (1 Corinthians 7:5)".

(Sandford, John and Paula, "The Transformation of the Inner Man", p 270, 273)

The word *"yada"* in Hebrew is the same word used for "knowing" God and "knowing" truth - it implies deep intimacy and means the same as sexual intercourse. God instituted the marriage covenant. It's mentioned many times in the Bible, repeating the same truth: *"For this reason, a man will leave his father and mother and be united to his wife, and they will become one flesh."* (Genesis 2:24; Matthew 19:4-6; 1 Corinthians 6:16; Ephesians 5:31)

Ungodly Sex and Ungodly Soul Ties

An ungodly soul tie is any unacceptable bonding that is contrary to God's plan and purpose for humanity. *An ungodly tie happens when a person submits to or is dominated by another.* In extreme cases, brainwashing techniques control and manipulate a person's mind and will. Fear of a person with whom you are in a relationship is a likely indicator that some form of ungodly domination is being exercised. *(Galatians 5 19-21; 1 John 2:11)*

The verb *"shakav"* in Hebrew merely means sexual intercourse, but it is used in most of the rape incidents. This term is the same word used to describe David's sexual act with Bathsheba.

2 Samuel 11: 4, *"Then David sent messengers to get her. She came to him, and he slept with her. (Now she was purifying herself from her monthly uncleanness.) Then she went back home."*

Ungodly sex is an expression of idolatry; read Bible verses, Numbers 25:1-3 and Romans 1:21-25. When a man or woman enters into an ungodly relationship that disregards marriage, sexual intercourse still remains a spiritual act of worship (an expression of the fulfillment of God's created purpose.) As there cannot be a spiritual vacuum, Satan moves on to the throne. Worship takes place, but instead of receiving the blessing of the Holy Spirit, demons enter as unclean spirits. The whole of Satanism is interwoven with idolatry and sexual intercourse.

"Israel's neighbors in ancient times actually incorporated adultery into their religious rites. Pagans worshiped their gods through cultic prostitution, believing that sex would put them in touch with divine power". (NIV Insight Bible)

In 1 Corinthians 6:18-20, Paul admonishes us to flee from sexual immorality:

"Flee from sexual immorality. All other sins a person commits are outside the body, but whoever sins sexually, sins against their own body. Do you not know that your bodies are temples of the Holy Spirit, who is in you, whom you have received from God? You are not your own; you were bought at a price. Therefore honor God with your bodies."

Sexual relationships outside the marriage covenant are *rebellion against God* and, therefore, cannot be under his spiritual covering. Where a couple has lived together before marriage, the subsequent marriage will not remove the fact of their sin. They will still need to acknowledge and confess it as a sin individually.

As all sexual intercourse involves body, soul, and spirit, a spiritual bond or soul tie will have been established with past sexual partners. Only God can break such soul ties, but until they are broken, they will continue to hold the couple in spiritual bondage even though marriage with a new partner may have taken place. So often, sexual sin has its *roots in the hurts and pain of the past.* Jesus did not condemn, nor do we condemn. With His love, we seek to bring healing and freedom.

Some Examples of Ungodly Soul Ties:

• Spending time with people with bad morals and picking up bad habits

1 Corinthians 15:33, *"Do not be misled, bad company corrupts good character."*

- Children with dominating, controlling parents
- Parents with undisciplined and manipulative children
- All relationships where there is ungodly dominance of one person over another
- With sexual partners in premarital and post-marital relationships
- All relationships that are abusive (through sexual, emotional, physical, or psychological manipulation)
- Through joining with submission to leaders and controlling pastors
- Unresolved grief with the dead
- A person unites with an occult practitioner (in cults, witchcraft, idols) through a spiritual connection and commits spiritual adultery, therefore forming a spiritual tie.

John Sandford wrote, *"Sex outside of marriage is ungodly sex, but it still forms a soul tie. It is a one-flesh bonding - a Biblical marriage is taking place. The couple's spirits and souls are being joined, but this time the Holy Spirit has no part in the union. The Holy Spirit will not flow in forbidden places!"* (p273)

Fornication leaves the way open for other spirits to become involved. Instead of bringing blessings, the enemy gains a foothold in our lives. God says, "I will not share my throne with another." We do not want to be in ungodly spiritual rebellion against the word of God!

In 1 Corinthians 6, Paul says,

"The body is not meant for sexual immorality, but for the Lord, and the Lord for the body...he who unites himself with the Lord is one with him in spirit. Flee from sexual immorality. All other sins that men or women commit are outside the body. But whoever sins sexually, sins against their own body. Do you not know that your body is the temple of the Holy Spirit who is in you, whom you have received from God? You are not your own, you were bought at a price. Therefore, honor and glorify God with your body."

So, we become one with the person we have sexual intercourse with, and if this is not our marriage partner, an ungodly soul tie is formed.

Ungodly sex comes in many forms:

- *Premarital sex* - sex before marriage with the intended partner or otherwise. Some say, "If we are going to marry anyway...?" The Bible still calls this fornication, so flee it. *(Read 1 Corinthians 5:1; 7:2; Ephesians 5:3; Colossians 3:5; 1 Thessalonians 4:3,4; Revelation 22:15)*

- *Trial marriage* - Sex with someone to see if you both are sexually compatible. Even if you decide you are not, you're still married in God's eyes. Trial sex creates trust issues in marriage because you can't trust your marriage partner to be faithful to you once you know they were willing to have sex with someone outside of "marriage," even if that person was you. You will wonder if the person would do it again or if you could trust them or even be trusted. Anything less than a public covenant is not enough. Secret, private agreements are not strong enough to overcome the heart's deceitfulness.

- *Cohabitation* - living together and having a sexual relationship while unmarried. The world today says this is not 'living in sin,' or even applauds 'living in sin' as evidence of being able to engage in life - uninhibited by 'evil' social constraints forcibly imposed by Christian' moralizers' by making one believe marriage is reduced to just a piece of paper and not a covenant created by God.

- *Incestual sex or marriage* - sex with forbidden family members and relatives. Bible scriptures *Leviticus 18 and 26* list the restrictions on incest. The harm done to children by incest is not created by an inconvenient social convention but is spiritual and emotional damage caused by violating the way we are made! *(Read Leviticus 18:6-18; Deuteronomy 27:22; Matthew 18:6)*

- *Adultery* - one or both parties are married to another person. In *Matthew 5:27-30,* Jesus makes it explicit and extends the idea of adultery from just a bodily joining to looking, lusting, and thinking. Adultery is committed to the heart, not just the body. Adultery and idolatry are closely related, even interchangeable, in the Old Testament, replacing worship of the one to whom it is due with worship of another.

Hebrews 13:4, *"Marriage should be honored by all, and the marriage bed kept pure, for God will judge the adulterer and all the sexually immoral."*

- *Prostitution* - apart from the destructive nature of sexual union with someone other than your spouse, the turning of sex into a business for monetary gain perverts every notion of God's intention for intimacy *(1 Corinthians 6:13-20)*.

- *Pornography, voyeurism, and fantasy* - immoral sexual activity enjoyed to stimulate erotic feelings. When pornography is consumed, you cannot expect to be negatively impacted by it. Pornography is very defiling and undermines intimacy with a marriage partner, reducing sex to the gratification of the flesh only. Pornography is very addictive, and prayer can be effective in breaking this addictive practice. Pornography fuels fantasy lust, and often, masturbation is also involved.

- *Masturbation or auto sexuality* - stimulating oneself for sexual pleasure or sexual attraction to oneself, especially a preference for masturbation over sexual intercourse. Many books, even Christian books, say masturbation is OK, a needed release for unfulfilled sexual tension. However, it is unhelpful for the believer because it is addictive and encourages fantasy, lust, and adultery in the heart. It opens a door through fantasy into the demonic, over which you lose control. Sex with self is based on lies, unreality, and false comfort. It is a progressive enemy strategy that starts innocently and worsens because it goes against God's plan for sex to be shared intimately between husband and wife. *(Read Proverbs 12:11b; Matthew 18:9; 1 Corinthians 6:13b)*

Galatians 5:19-21, *The acts of the flesh are obvious: sexual immorality, impurity and debauchery; idolatry and witchcraft; hatred, discord, jealousy, fits of rage, selfish ambition, dissensions, factions and envy; drunkenness, orgies, and the like. I warn you, as I did before, that those who live like this will not inherit the kingdom of God."*

- *Bestiality* - having sex with animals. This kind of sex opens the possibilities for spiritual bonding and demon spirits, which the Bible often associates with various animal forms. Sex with animals carries a **curse**; therefore, certainly, the Holy Spirit is not present.

Deuteronomy 27:21, *"Cursed is anyone who has sexual relations with any animal."*
Then all the people shall say, "Amen!"

• *Sexual abuse and rape* - any act of sexual contact that a person suffers or performs as a result of force, fear, or without having legally consented to the act. This ungodly soul tie is widespread and takes many forms. *(Deuteronomy 22:23; 2 Samuel 13:12-15)*

• *Sadistic and masochistic sex* - willfully participating in acts that involve humiliation, physical abuse, and bondage for gratification. This kind of sex is becoming more common in our world today and is linked with perversion and fantasy.

Why Break a Soul Tie?

Here are examples of when it is imperative to break ungodly soul ties:

• If domination and intimidation cause fear for their safety, they must break ties with their abuser.

• If they are *married*, they must break ties with anyone they have had sexual contact with in the past or currently.

• If they are struggling with addiction, they must break ties with anyone who tempts them to stay in an unhealthy lifestyle.

If they are not obligated to stay in the relationship, they can break the tie entirely and never see the person again. Even if they must remain in a relationship on some level, such as with an ex with whom they share custody of the children or their parents, there is a way to experience freedom from the person's control over them.

Here are some questions to ask them about the friendships, past and present, that they are struggling with:

• Do I feel confined and restricted in this relationship?

• Am I sticking it out only because I am afraid of being alone?

• Are my thoughts about the situation obsessive and out of control?

• Am I unable to sleep, plagued with nightmares, or unable to eat because of this relationship?

If they answered these questions with a "yes," then their friendship kept them from being the person they were created to be. They need to let go so there will be room for better, healthier relationships.

Breaking a soul tie is especially important for ex-boyfriends and ex-girlfriends. Their current relationships, including marriages, will suffer if they carry those relationships in their hearts and invest emotional energy into them. They are tempted to think that no one will be hurt if they do not talk about their past and no one knows about their private thoughts. But their attachment to the past is robbing them of fulfillment in what they have now.

How to Break a Soul Tie

1. If any sins were committed to cause this soul tie, repent of them! Fornication is perhaps one of the most common ways to create nasty soul ties, so repent of any sins committed.

2. If gifts were given by the other person in connection with the sin or unholy relationship, such as rings, flowers, cards, lingerie, etc., get rid of them! Such things symbolize the ungodly relationship and can hold a soul tie in place; therefore, it must be destroyed.

3. Any rash vows or commitments that formed the soul tie should be renounced, repented, and broken in Jesus' name. Even statements and inner vows like *"I will love you forever"* or *"I could never love another man!"* must be renounced and undone verbally. The tongue can bring significant troubles and bondage to the soul.

As Proverbs 21:23 tells us, *"Whoso keepeth his mouth and his tongue keepeth his soul from troubles."*

4. Forgive that person if you have anything against them.

5. Renounce the soul tie.

6. There may be a need for deliverance and prayer to heal the human spirit. There may also be a need for Godly confrontation and ending any ongoing ungodly relationship.

Prayer to Break Ungodly Soul Ties

Verbally say this prayer out loud:

"In Jesus' name I now make a voluntary decision to break all ungodly soul ties that have been established between _____ and myself and I renounce AND break and sever any ungodly soul ties formed between myself and _____ as a result of _____ (fornication, drugs, prostitution, adultery etc.) and I cancel all legal rights held by Satan. I ask You, Father, to take away all that _____ has placed upon me of his/her personality and control, and cleanse me from all defilement and guilt received through that relationship, in the name of Jesus. In Jesus name, I also close any doors that were left open to the occult realm, and I hide _____ in You, God. I speak to every demonic spirit that has taken advantage of this ungodly soul tie and command you to go. I release _____ to You, Lord, I plead the Blood of Jesus over myself and _____ and I place the cross of Christ between us. I choose now to surrender myself to You, my only Lord and Savior. In Jesus' Name, Amen."

Renew the mind with the word of God Ps 124: 7,8, "_I have escaped like a bird out of the fowler's snare; the snare IS broken, and I have escaped. My help is in the name of the Lord, maker of heaven and earth._"

***If you are praying this prayer with someone, allow time for God to go deep and do the work that needs to be done. There may be sobbing, groanings that cannot be uttered, and even falling to the floor. Do not be alarmed. Stay calm, pray in the Holy Ghost, and let God do HIS perfect work in them.

Sexual Abuse

Sexual abuse is one of the most common issues dealt with in inner healing ministries, yet it is one of the most sensitive subjects. Most of those reporting abuse are females, and there is a thought that it is because males are too proud to say anything.

Although this lesson deals with abusers in general, this lesson will lean toward the sexual abuser. Sexual abusers are often charming, intelligent people who serve as teachers, Scout leaders, daycare workers, and ministers. Although they may be completely sincere in their Conscious desires to help others, they are more deeply and powerfully motivated by the need to find well-being and fulfillment through the ones they seek to serve.

This lesson offers a general description of the history and character of a potential sexual abuser. Those who fit many aspects of this profile, who have never become abusers, should praise God and ask Him to heal areas of vulnerability with the power of the cross. Those who seek to minister to abusers may begin to respond with increased understanding and compassion, not to excuse their sin, but to be prepared to help them deal with it at the root level.

Symptoms of sexual abuse are similar to symptoms of other traumas, but even at that, it is imperative to be cautious and never assume. Paul Sanford, in her book, "Healing Victims of Sexual Abuse" (Tulsa, OK: Victory House, 1988), lists some of the symptoms of sexual abuse in the lives of adults:

- Recurrent and intrusive collections: dreams or reliving of experiences that indicate abuse
- Generalized anxiety, mistrust, and social isolation
- Difficulty forming or maintaining non-exploitative intimate relationships
- Sexual dysfunction
- Chronic depression, self-blame, and poor self-esteem

- Depressive symptoms
- Avoiding certain people or situations out of fear, even when unrelated to the abuse
- Diminished self-protection, masochistic strivings, and repeated victimization; may injure(cut) or mutilate self or become involved in substance abuse
- Identity focused on a sense of "badness" and stigmatization.
- Contempt for women, including herself
- Tendency to fear men, but also to overvalue and idealize certain men as well-know
- Involvement in promiscuity or prostitution
- Emotional numbness
- Inappropriate guilt; underlying anger and resentment

The Short-term and Long-term Effects of Sexual Abuse:

- *Overwhelming confusion:* A sense of betrayal-particularly if the abuser is a trusted authority figure
- *Inability to trust:* They feel like the authority figures in their lives did not protect them, and they judge God and others as unworthy of their trust. They keep to themselves, do not form close relationships, and develop strong defense mechanisms to protect themselves.
- *Confused and distorted identity:* this is most acute when it is the victim's father since she was forced to relate to him in a way that should have been reserved for her mother; her father did not treat her as his beloved daughter who was worthy of pure love, affection, and protection but treated her in a way that left her feeling betrayed, undervalued, dirty, shameful, manipulated and used.
- *Guilt and shame:* Many victims of sexual abuse think they are the ones responsible for the abuse they have experienced. They think they did something wrong, or that they had the power to stop it, or that there is something wrong with them. On the one hand, they did not like the things their abuser did- they were strange, dirty, or disgusting, or the victim enjoyed the attention and intimacy and went along with it. Her body probably responded to the stimulation involved in the abuse.

- *Anger, bitterness, and a desire for revenge:* toward the perpetrator, toward her parents; why did they let this happen? Why would you marry that man? Why didn't Mom stop it?

- *Toward God:* anger toward God is often present in the hearts of victims of sexual abuse. Where was God when I needed Him? God did not protect me, so the only one I can count on is me.

- *Toward Others:* loathing and criticism of classmates and church members; deeply rooted ambivalence toward parents, a desperate need for love, feeling ruined, feelings of inferiority, a need to get even, a need to prove the truth of the judgment she has made against men,(men are all alike, all they want is sex) and an out-of-control sex drive.

- *Thoughts of death and suicide as well as susceptibility to drug and alcohol abuse:* death may seem preferable to the emotional pain she experiences, drawn to drugs, alcohol, and self-mutilation.

- *Sexual difficulties in marriage:* She automatically shuts down in the middle of lovemaking, or she survived the abuse by fantasizing, and now, as an adult, she automatically begins fantasizing during sex with her husband.

The good news is unhealthy soul ties can be broken and ungodly sexual activity can be forgiven. If we have sinned, Jesus promises to forgive us of our sins when we repent. If we were violated or sinned against, we can ask the Lord to help us forgive our offender and ask Jesus to cleanse us. He can restore the purity and innocence stolen from us.

A Prayer to Heal from Sexual Abuse

Lord, thank you for your Son Jesus and His shed blood on the cross. I come out of agreement with all unhealthy soul ties and sexual abuse with _____. I forgive _____ for what they did and how it has affected me and those connected to me. Forgive me, for any part I played in this sexual abuse. I give back to _____ everything I may have taken from them, and I take back everything _____ took from me, including from my heart. I renounce and break this unhealthy soul tie of sexual abuse with _____, and I release myself from them. I am free and no longer in bondage from the sexual abuse.

I renounce and cancel all darkness associated with this ungodly soul tie. I decree and declare that I am completely healed, restored, and purified through Jesus' blood. I pray _____ is healed and restored too. Lord, I ask you to remove all hurtful past memories and give me memories of joy, peace, and hope. I pray blessings on _____ because they are your child too.

Thank you for healing me, In Jesus Name, Amen.

Healing After an Abortion, Miscarriage, and Stillbirth

Spirits of sin are spirits that lodge themselves in people because of specific sins they have committed. Spirits do not enter because you have sinned. When you sin over a prolonged period of time, you are disregarding the will of God and moving away from His protection. It is worth mentioning that when a woman has an abortion, *"a spirit called" abortion" sometimes enters the woman or the doctor"* (Francis MacNutt, Deliverance from Evil Spirits, pg. 200) . We want to make sure we pray with any women for healing of post-abortion trauma.

Abortion is known to bring emotional torment in its aftermath, yet few understand this as being demonic and spiritual bondage. Abortion, as far as the Bible is concerned, is nothing less than the murder of an innocent person that God has created and is a source of great spiritual bondage.

What makes abortion murder?

The token that the pro-choice uses is that the fetus (unborn child) is not a person yet but only a mass of tissue. (For that matter, many today also believe that we evolved from apes and are nothing more than a mass of tissue ourselves!) If the fetus were simply a mass of tissue without a human spirit, then I think we could justify abortion. However, the fetus is not merely a mass of tissue but rather a person to whom God is knitting together their physical body in the mother's womb. If the fetus was simply a useless mass of tissue, then abortion may be excusable.

However, if the unborn child happens to be a natural person whose body is growing together in its mother's womb, then abortion is nothing less than the murder of an innocent life. Just because the unborn child's body is still being knit together does not mean they are not yet human. Children are not fully developed until they are 18, but we would never consider them any less than human beings!

At what point does the spirit join with the body?

At what point does the baby (whether born or unborn) become a human possessing a spirit? Does this happen when the child is 18 years old and is said to be an adult? Does this happen when the child says their first words? How do we know when this happens? We could assume it takes place at the age of 18, which would make it seem okay to kill anybody under eighteen. That would be silly, wouldn't it? Who is to say that the baby is not an actual human until it leaves the womb? This argument is what the pro-choice believes, but do they have any proof of this? Can it be backed with scripture? Absolutely not! It is nothing more than an assumption that they are incapable of backing with any evidence! Nowhere in the entire Bible does it give us even a hint that the child does not become a human being with a spirit until it leaves the womb!

Luke 2:21, *"And when eight days were accomplished for the circumcising of the child, his name was called JESUS, which was so named of the angel before he was conceived in the womb."*

2 Kings 4:17, *"And the woman conceived and bore a son at that season that Elisha had said unto her, according to the time of life."*

If you take the word 'conceive' in the above verse and look it up in its Hebrew roots, we are given the Hebrew word *harah*, which is interpreted to: *"A primitive root; to be (or become) pregnant, conceive (literally or figuratively): – been, be with child, conceive, progenitor."* For a woman to conceive literally means she is now with a child. Yet, pro-choicers want us to believe that when a woman is pregnant, it is not a child, but just a mass of tissue! This claim sounds similar to those who think we came from apes and are still just a mass of tissue ourselves!

An unborn child is still a person in the eyes of God: The Bible is clear that God formed us in our mother's womb, and He knew us before we were even conceived.

Jeremiah 1:5 says, *"Before I formed you in the womb I knew you, before you were born I set you apart; I appointed you as a prophet to the nations."*

Satan is no dummy when it comes to deceiving the world. He is pretty famous for his clever deception. Some women experience little or no torment after having abortions. Still, I believe they are 'spared' to deceive the rest of us that it is okay to have abortions and that not all women will be tormented afterward. Wouldn't it make sense if Satan keeps 3% of those women who have abortions to be examples of how not all women are tormented after having an abortion so that they could tell the rest of us how they have not been negatively affected by their abortion. Do not fall for Satan's clever deception.

If a "fetus" (unborn child) was simply a mass of tissue, then it would be impossible for any woman who believes such a lie to experience such awful mental torment and shame after having an abortion. The truth is abortion is a source of enormous spiritual and mental bondage and torment. It is a means for spiritual defilement, just as cold-blooded murder is, and opens a person up to unclean spirits (demons) to enter and harass the person. Studies have shown that abortion is also linked to suicide because of the torment and bondage. Many women feel that it's better they were not even born if they have to face such torment. Nobody knows what it is like to be in bondage until they are the ones facing it in their own lives, and the sad truth is that many women today do not realize what they are getting themselves into until it is too late and the damage is already done.

Women who have had abortions almost always experience some or many of the following symptoms:

- Bondage to shame and guilt
- Nightmares relating to the abortion
- Feeling that God would never forgive them
- Depression, which can lead to suicide (Studies show that abortion is linked to suicide)
- Self-hatred for allowing themselves to do such a thing
- Sleep disorders – finding it hard to get to sleep at night
- Flashbacks and even hearing sounds of children crying
- Desire to have another baby to replace the aborted baby
- Inability to form a true loving bond with her other children

The list of side effects from an abortion is long. Jesus made it clear that murder is a means for defilement and opens the door to unclean spirits to come in and play havoc in a person's life. I believe behind every case of suicide is a demonic spirit that drives the person to take their own life to end the pain they are facing. People who have come close to suicide will often admit that there was a force that was 'driving' them to take their own life. It often tells them they could end their problems by pulling the plug.

The linkage between abortions and suicide:

• Abortion is nothing less than murder and opens the door to spirits that will drive a person into the ground, allowing sinful spirits to enter. Depression is a common side effect that is experienced by those who have had an abortion. It is common for this depression to affect the person so severely that they are driven to suicide.

• Suicide is almost, if not always, caused by a demonic spirit. When a woman has been defiled through murder, they're now open to a murder-related spirit of suicide. *The relative risk for self-harm among the aborting group of his study cohort was 1.7, i.e., they were 70% more likely to self-harm than the non-aborting group. Similarly, Speckhard's study of thirty women post-abortion found that 65% had suicide ideation and 31% had attempted suicide."* (https://thelifeinstitute.net/learning-centre/abortion-effects/suicide-after-abortion)   The world wants you to think it's your body to do as you please, but this is false. Your body was bought with a price and no longer belongs to you.

1 Corinthians 6:20, *"For ye are bought with a price: therefore glorify God in your body, and in your spirit, which are God's."*

Inner Healing from Abortion's Aftermath

The numbers are staggering—almost 1 out of 3 women in America has had an abortion. The chances are that you, or someone you know well, maybe one of those women. We believe in the grace of Jesus and are firmly convinced that God is a great Redeemer, and no sin excludes us from the forgiveness and healing found in Him alone. There is also NO judgment here for those who have had one. There is only honor and love!

The good news for those who have had an abortion is that they can be forgiven and set free from the aftermath of it. It is almost always necessary that such individuals go through deliverance to rid themselves of any unclean spirits that they have picked up, tear down strongholds that have come on the scene, receive quality post-deliverance discipleship, and maintain a healthy relationship with God so that they can receive and hold on to their freedom. It may be possible to receive a measure of freedom without a deliverance, but I would never bypass this step if I had an abortion in my background. It is possible to experience a false sense of freedom without dealing with the root, but in such cases, they will remain in bondage somehow, and it just does not go away. If unclean spirits are involved, then the partial freedom that they find will continue to be challenged and fought for as the spirits continue to work on the person to pull them down and torment them.

There are numerous psychological and medical terms describing a woman's grief following an abortion. One of the results of abortion may be endometriosis: endometrial-like cells appear and flourish in areas outside the uterine cavity, most commonly on the ovaries, because it has to do with hormonal interruption. From Post Abortion Syndrome to PTSD, the fact is that an abortion is not just a medical procedure, as many would want us to believe. No, this choice affects a woman's soul at the deepest levels. A woman is designed to protect her womb, and when violence has occurred against her child, it strikes her at the very core of her being. As a result, many women are left to deal with the resulting violation in silence. Some are silent out of shame, and others from pressure by pro- choice groups who want us to pretend there are no consequences to this perceived "right", but know that through inner healing, they will be honored and receive the love of Christ that will heal them.

1. BELIEVE HEALING IS POSSIBLE:

When I think of Jesus, my mind not only goes to my own experiences of profound mercy, but I cannot help but think of the number of women in scripture who discovered unconditional love and grace in Him. These women were outcasts from their communities and carried tremendous cultural shame, but in the eyes of Jesus, they found forgiveness. Let us never forget that Jesus is God, who came to dwell among us, to make us new, and to bind up our wounds.

Psalm 147:3, *"He heals the brokenhearted and binds up their wounds."*

2. BRING THEIR SECRET INTO THE LIGHT:

A dear friend sat down and talked to me before she and her husband moved to Hawaii. After taking my Beauty for Ashes class for inner healing at another church, she had an abortion while she was married and wanted to be free of her pain and shame. She was also a new believer and told me, *"I am learning that healing is a process, and, in many ways, I think I am still in that process. My journey to healing began when I brought the secret into the light, had the courage to sign up for your class and actually showed up. As long as I kept it a secret, Satan was using it to accuse me and to speak accusations over me. When I brought it into the light and confessed it to trusted friends and pastors who love Jesus, then I was able to begin my journey of healing."* God not only healed her but gave her two more very beautiful and healthy children after that abortion! She and her husband live in North Carolina and have a beautiful, healed relationship because she is no longer in bondage from the secret she kept hidden once it was brought into the light.

Repentance is required to bring the truth to the light, to cast out the spirit of abortion, along with other companion spirits of various sexual sins, including the spirit of murder and depression.

When you let Jesus' light, His truth, penetrate the hidden places and drive out the darkness, you will be filled with more light.

In John 3:19-20 it says, *"And the judgment is based on this fact: God's light came into the world, but people loved the darkness more than the light, for their actions were evil. All who do evil hate the light and refuse to go near it for fear their sins will be exposed. But those who do what is right come to the light so others can see that they are doing what God wants."*

Prayer After Abortion, Miscarriage, and StillBirth

Here are the steps to follow and pray as the Holy Spirit leads:

1. Pray and confess the sin, repent, and ask God for forgiveness for the sin of murder.

2. Pray for the healing of any guilt, shame, fear, and confusion that existed at the time of the abortion.

3. If necessary, pray that Jesus will come into the experience.

4. Pray a prayer of committal for release (the mother frees her soul tied to the child, and also releases the child to Jesus, committing the baby for whatever good purposes He has in store for the baby).

5. Pray the Lord brings peace between mother and child.

6. Pray for healing of any guilt involved.

7. Pray that the mother may see the child with Jesus (the Lord may reveal the child's sex.)

8. Sometimes, the Lord will reveal the child's name; if not, have the mother name the child.

9. Pray a blessing upon the mother and the child.

10. Pray that what is loosed on earth is loosed in heaven (Matt 16:19)

11. If possible and applicable, have both parents pray to forgive themselves. (During this prayer, the grief may come out as either anger or deep hurt, and there may be much sobbing, which is part of the release process.)

12. Pray a prayer for cleansing and pray that every female organ and tissue works and operates perfectly and correctly, exactly the way God created them to operate.

It is essential that you renew your mind to the Word after praying for healing. Again, if you do not, the enemy of your soul will come at them with new accusations and guilt.

Father Wounds

We all come into the world helpless, dependent, and needing acceptance to be treated as worthy and blessed. The father's wound is the absence of this agape love from your birth father. That wound can be caused by:

- Neglect – I am unimportant
- Absence – Divorce, separation, death
- Abuse – Mental, physical, sexual, spiritual
- Control – Oppressive domination
- Withholding – Love, blessings, or affirmation, deficiencies that lead to a profound lack of self-acceptance.

The effect of a father wound is low self-esteem, deep emotional pain inside, and a performance orientation that makes you "doers" rather than "beings." While salvation makes you a new creation in Christ, it does not necessarily address the wound inside. Below are four barriers that inhibit the healing of this wound:

- Pride – No will to confront or change, "I'm alright."
- Sin – A blocked will that neither seeks to confess sin nor receive forgiveness
- The wound itself – Continuous emotional hurt inside
- Lies – Misconceptions about the Self, birth father, and Father God.

Instead of going through the pain and receiving the healing you need, you tend to respond to life events by creating a misconception about yourself.

Relationship to the Birth Father

When you hold a conception of your birth father as angry, violent, uncaring, indifferent, distant/withdrawn, absent/abandoning, alcoholic, condemning, and critical, you tend to believe the following words about yourself:

- I am unworthy
- I am stupid
- I am incompetent
- I am unloved or unlovable

As long as you accept these words as truth, you will experience a depressed, anxious, and angry life.

Relationship to God the Father

Often, a person's image of God the Father is contaminated by the personal experience they have with their birth father. When misconceptions about God are present (i.e., that He is angry, judgmental, unhappy with me, fearsome, legalistic, quick to punish and slow to forgive), the words one tends to believe are:

- I am not good enough
- I am guilty/shameful
- I must work harder to justify myself

As long as you accept these words as truth, you perform and prove your worth through perfectionism and materialism or seek addictions to cover up the pain.

Addressing the Father's Wound

There are four steps to addressing the father's wound:

1. Understanding the heart of God
2. Inviting Jesus into the wounds created by the birth father
3. Accepting the truth about oneself as a child of God
4. The heart of God

As seen in the Prodigal Son story:
- you are free to choose your path
- patiently, The Father waits for you to return to Him

- when you return, He accepts you unconditionally
- He runs to accept and embrace you
- He values you by celebrating God's provision for salvation
- He loves you first
- You are His beloved creation
- He offers salvation for your sin
- He desires a relationship with you

Jesus as the Wounded Healer:

- He was tempted by Satan to know your temptations
- He experienced suffering to know your suffering
- He was rejected, mocked, beaten, and crucified
- He fully understands your pain and wants to help

1 Peter 2:24, *"By His wounds you have been healed."*

Jesus Heals:

- when invited into your memories, He comes
- when He comes into the memories, He is described as gentle, kind, caring, loving, warm, friendly, smiling, hugging, accepting, and healing.

When you understand His love:

- confess to Him the misconception you have had
- receive His forgiveness
- receive His love

Invite Jesus into the Wounds Created by Your Birth Father

Do inner healing for the memories:

- invite Jesus into the specific memories
- understand the words that you accepted at the time
- ask Jesus to reveal His truth to you
- receive His truth about who you are

Choose to forgive your birth father:

- for hurtful words
- for hurtful actions
- for not loving you
- for not blessing you
- for affecting your image of God, the Father

Accept Yourself as a Child of God

Receive the words of truth from God's word:

- I am accepted
- I am chosen (Ephesians 1:11)
- I am loved (Lamentations 3:22-23)
- I am God's creation (Ephesians 2:10)
- I am precious in His sight (Isaiah 43:4)
- I am forgiven (Psalm 103)
- I have been redeemed (Isaiah 44:21-22)
- I will never be forsaken (Hebrews 13:5)
- I have an eternal inheritance (1 Peter 1:3-9)
- nothing can separate me from the love of God (Romans 8:31-39)

As you understand the truth about God's love and come to know your True Self in Christ, it will free you to let go of the pain and forgive your birth father. This new perspective will now enable you to see your birth father through different eyes and help you to live in freedom.

How does "the father wound" impact adult well-being and relationships?

- **Low self-esteem & low confidence:** You often blame yourself for anything negative that happened in childhood, especially if it was not explained to you.

- **Anxiety:** There could be a combination of things and events that have contributed to you experiencing anxiety. Growing up with an (emotionally) absent father may have left you with a feeling of *"I am not good enough,"* and perhaps you have hidden feelings such as a sense of loss, anger, shame, sadness; and anxiety is trying to keep those deeper emotions at bay.

- **Low mood/depression:** Over time, your anxiety can turn to low mood. On the other hand, you may have internalized your anger towards your father for being absent and feel depressed as a result.

- **Anger & Rage:** Perhaps you have had the worst experience with your father. Maybe he used substances and was an abusive, lying, and otherwise unreliable man whose behavior deeply hurt you. You feel stuck in anger, which can manifest in many ways: rage, bitterness, mean attitudes, fighting, rudeness, etc.

- **Too rigid boundaries:** If your father has been unreliable, perhaps by not showing up or even being absent from your life, you may have decided that you cannot let people (romantic partners) close to you, and you must protect yourself.

- **Too loose boundaries:** You may feel you must always be available to everyone else. Perhaps deep down, you feel that to be loved by others, you cannot hold your boundaries and say "no" when something does not suit you.

- **Having relationships with emotionally unavailable partners:** Unless you are aware of it, you often seek the same dynamic in your romantic relationships as you experienced in childhood. Relationships may be complicated because the men may show an interest, yet as the women attach and show interest in them, they disappear or withdraw from contact using various excuses.

- **Often choosing emotionally unavailable partners:** You may experience a lot of relationship anxiety when your partner is unable to offer you the security you need and long for, so you often end up engaging in various behaviors to get their attention, such as nagging, excessive messaging, oversharing, or needy behaviors that may feel unsettling for your partner.

- **Parenting – repeating the pattern of (emotionally) absent parent:** When you first become a parent, and you're flooded with feelings that may be linked to your own experiences of being parented or experiencing a lack of parenting, repeating the same behaviors, language, and mindset

If at all possible, once you've realized what "emotional hurt" you've been experiencing, go back and revisit the places of your old emotional wounds. Most of all, you need to see God as a loving Heavenly Father who only wants the best for you and would never turn His back on His child. This view of Him may have been grossly distorted through your eyes. Just as Joyce Meyer had written in her book Beauty for Ashes about walking back through those doors of pain, this may be necessary for a daughter to heal from a father's wound. I won't lie---it can be difficult and "almost" impossible for a daughter to heal from her father's wounds because there is a significant, powerful, spiritual component that is tied to a father's role, influence, and impact. When coupled with dark spiritual forces that want this relationship to stay "unhealed," it can do a number on destroying or cluttering the daughter's relationship with God as her Dad. If Dad agrees with restoring the relationship, I suggest going through an Inner Healing session. If the pain from the father's wound is still there after an inner healing session, we use our discretion as the Holy Spirit speaks and will refer you to long-term counseling alongside your inner healing journey.

If you experienced childhood emotional neglect, it is a strong possibility you may repeat the pattern as you don't know any difference. Maybe you have become a practical parent and struggle to engage with your child(ren) emotionally.

Fathers need to understand because they are the ones who shape their daughter's understanding and perception of God as a Father, how they respond to their daughters influences how they react forever to Father God. If your horizontal relationship is damaged and unhealed, it will be nearly impossible to respond to the vertical relationship with Jesus. Fathers need to live out the truth in Psalms 103:13:

"The LORD is like a father to his children, tender and compassionate to those who fear him."

Their compassion must be a true reflection of the Lord's compassion for His children. Father God can heal you from all father wounds as His love can drench you with unconditional, restorative, live-giving love.

Prayer for Father Wounds

Heavenly Father, I confess I hold unforgiveness in my heart towards my dad. Please forgive me. I choose to forgive my father for all the hurt and pain he caused me knowingly and unknowingly. I release him of the debt I feel I'm owed. Please help me to experience freedom from all bitterness, anger, and resentment I hold inside. Lord, show me your love and fill every void missing in my life with Your truth and what Your word says about me.

Mother Wounds

We all come into the world needing the tender presence of a mother's touch, nurture, care, and love. The mother's influence begins when we are in the womb. The absence of this mother's love is a wound that is created in three ways:

1. The mother is separated from the child through:

1. Illness of the mother
2. Mother's death
3. Divorce

2. *The child is separated from the mother through:*

1. Illness Of The Child
2. Incubator/Hospitalization
3. Adoption

3. *Unhappy relationship with mother through:*

1. Neglect
2. Abuse
3. Mother's Mental And Emotional Distress
4. Attempted Abortion

When this most important attachment is traumatically interrupted, emotional pain produces consequences within the individual. The effects of the wounding include:

- Feelings of abandonment and dread of aloneness
- Loss of self and sense of being
- Powerful hunger for a feminine touch that can be eroticized
- Emotional dependencies
- Possible gender confusion, fear, and insecurity

There are two primary responses to a mother wound that affects one's ability to achieve healthy friendships and healthy married love:

1. Emotional detachment – This defensive response to the breakdown in the mother's love causes a detachment from the mother. The legitimate need for love from the mother is repressed, leaving the child hungry but unable to secure relationships because of the emotional shutdown. You fear the pain of attachment and build protective walls to hide behind.

2. Emotional dependency – In this response, you strive endlessly to fill the void, which often turns into co-dependency with grasping, clutching, and infantile(childish) tendencies. Their striving for attachment is based on low self-confidence, fear, insecurity, and often confusion about self-worth.

Implications for Women

- internalize a low view of women
- addictive, emotional, and romantic dependencies
- infantile desire for union with women
- sexual confusion related to touch

Implications for Men

- ambivalence towards women – need them but very wary
- fixate on feminine objects of desire to fill the deprivation of mother love
- either detach or remain in the toxic grip of a sinful alliance with mother
- sexual confusion related to touch

Other implications

- separation anxiety that leads to striving, passivity, and depression
- fantasy bonding – attaching to fantasies
- fetish bonding – attaching to things, clothing, hair
- attachment to self – fantasy image of self
- emotional incest – meeting the emotional needs of the mother
- weak sense of identity and of being

Addressing the Mother's Wound

There are four steps to addressing the mother's wound:

1. Invite Jesus into your initial memories and emotions

2. Release the pain to Jesus and stop living from the center of your wounded child

3. Forgive their mother

4. Strengthen your sense of identity and knowledge of your True Self in Christ

> ➤ **Inviting Jesus into the Wound**

"Though my father and mother forsake me, the Lord will receive me."(Psalm 27:10)

"As a mother comforts her child, so I will comfort you." (Isaiah 66:13)

Knowing that Jesus wants to heal all who are broken-hearted, invite Jesus to enter into the place of your brokenness – in the womb, at birth, early in life, wherever it happens.

> ➤ **Release the painful memories to Jesus**

Ask Jesus to take away the pain in each painful memory and replace it with His love. He will creatively remove the pain (the "how" often differs for each person) and then transform the memory with His love and truth.

> ➤ **Forgive your Mother**

Choose to forgive your mother and let go of all the resentment, bitterness, and anger. Jesus' transforming love will change the perspective of the trauma and free you to accept the circumstances with grace and mercy.

> ➤ **Strengthen your sense of identity and knowledge of your True Self in Christ**

Ask Jesus to reveal the truth about who you are. As Jesus affirms your sense of being, He assures you of your worth and helps you know the True Self that He created.

As you connect with Jesus' profound love for you, the need for other attachments reduces your need to be loved and allows you to look outward at loving relationships with others. Living with your new self and being open to affirmation will free you to grow in your own story instead of constantly striving to attach to your mother or your substitute mother.

> ### _Prayer for Mother's Wounds_
>
> Lord, I invite you into my heart and every place I've hidden from you. I am surrendering it all to you. I confess my sins, hatred, dislike, and dishonoring my parents - even if they were dishonorable towards me. I repent of every word, thought, and action against my mother that was not pleasing in your hands. Lord, fill every void and and lack with your agape love.
>
> I am choosing to forgive my mom today and release all my hurt to you including bitterness and resentment. Lord, please heal all my damaged emotions and release me from any bondage from the devil. Remove every wrong thought and image of my mother and show me the truth about your daughter. Help me create healthy boundaries while I'm on this healing journey. I am removing myself from the judgment seat and letting You be the Judge. Lord, I pray you drown me and my mom in Your love and make us drunk in Your love because she too is your child.
>
> _In Jesus Name, I pray. Amen_

"In Utero"(WOMB) Wounds

The act of intercourse may be loving, but a resulting conception may be unwanted thus creating in utero wounds. If the mother, although not exclusively, has negative emotions when she realizes she is pregnant and continues her rejection of the child in her womb, then the spirit of the child will sense what is going on and begin to feel that rejection.

When you mention "memories," your thoughts usually relate to the things that have happened to you since birth. But quite often, the things that people react to the most are the moments that occurred while in the womb. We can see that there can be a lot of damage done before birth or "in utero." Helping people through "in utero" experiences is beneficial if you were conceived out of wedlock, or to those parents who wanted a child of the opposite sex that they got, or those who were experiencing financial difficulty or marital discord during the pregnancy. Many critics of this idea suggest that since they cannot recall early memories, the memories cannot influence them. This attitude is both wrong and dangerous. There is plenty of evidence that memories are very influential whether you can recall them or not. A University of California professor, John T. Noonan, explains that by the time the gestation process has reached two ½ months and could be much sooner, babies are experiencing life and recording those experiences in their brains. Dr. Thomas Verny, MD., a secular obstetrician and author of *"The Secret Life of the Unborn Child" says, "The womb is a child's first world. How he experiences it- free or hostile- creates personality and character predispositions. The womb establishes the child's expectations. If it has a warm, loving environment, the child will likely expect the outside world to be the same."* Unborn children are likely to pick up on any rejection, anger, fear, dissatisfaction, or resentment the mother is carrying and will interpret those emotions as being directed at them, whether that is the intent or not. There are many types of situations in which parents may signal rejection to their unborn child. Rejection is first felt in the womb by a child who was conceived out of wedlock or whose parents wanted the opposite sex.

Some doors that can be opened before or during birth:

- Remembers music played only during pregnancy

- Languages spoken by mother three months before birth.

- Unhappy and rejected babies have vast numbers of physical and behavioral problems.

- Fear and distress in the mother will result in immediate wild kicking of the baby, e.g., increased fetal kicking 10-fold at the death of the father in a car accident.

- The unborn child knows the voice of their mother and father.

- A fraction of a second after fear sets the mother's heart racing, the infant's rate will double.

- Fear of responsibility and fear of bearing a defective child raise the chances substantially of spontaneous abortion.

- Babies whose mothers smoked 40 or more cigarettes per day were born smaller and in poorer physical condition, with more reading problems at age six and more psychological disorders.

- Troubled moms have more complications in childbirth, such as: prolonged labor, poor attitude toward motherhood, poor relationship with the mother, and chronic anxieties, worries, and fears.

- Anxiety-filled, fearful women have problem bonding, higher birth complications, most prolonged labors, and most forceps-attempted deliveries.

When a mother strokes, hugs, and bonds with their child in as little as an hour after birth, it makes a critical difference. It creates better mothers and healthier babies physically, emotionally, and intellectually. By the 8th week in the womb, the baby scratches its nose, sucks its thumb, raises his head, and reaches out. They have individual and unique brain waves as early as the 5th week. Everything a mother thinks, feels, says, or hopes influences her unborn child.

We have ministered in several sessions to "in utero" memories where the mother and father had verbalized to their child of either being the wrong sex, a not-wanted pregnancy, or aborting them. Our receivers have dealt with such things throughout their lives as rejection, severe anxiety, not feeling wanted or good enough most of their lives, and didn't understand why. When we asked Jesus to walk them back to when Mom was pregnant with them and reveal the truth, He did, and Holy Spirit so lovingly and beautifully brought healing. It is a good idea to go back to the section on rejection if you believe you have things that you have dealt with "in utero" and allow Holy Spirit to show you what was said or what was done and how you need to be healed.

The Bible is the foundation, focus and filter of Inner Healing and Freedom. The goal is to ALWAYS take you back to the BLOOD and the CROSS.........without them we can not have healing.

In Psalm 139:13-16, it says *"For you formed my inward parts; you knitted me together in my mother's womb. I praise you, for I am fearfully and wonderfully made. Wonderful are your works; my soul knows it very well. My frame was not hidden from you, when I was being made in secret, intricately woven in the depths of the earth. Your eyes saw my unformed substance; in your book were written, every one of them, the days that were formed for me, when as yet there was none of them."*

Make this Your Personal Prayer

Father, I thank you for your Son Jesus who died on the cross not only for my sins, but for my hurts and for my fears. I thank you that Jesus is the same yesterday, today and forever, and that He wants me to be completely whole: mind, soul, body, and spirit. Lord Jesus, I ask you to walk back through every second of my life, to heal me and to make me whole. Go back into the third and fourth generations and break all harmful genetic ties.

Jesus, you knew all about me even before I was born. Thank you for being there as life began. If fear or any other negative force was transmitted to me as I was in my mother's womb, set me free from those things. Thank you, Lord Jesus, for being there when I was born, and for loving me. (If you came into this world not being loved or wanted, and felt such rejection, ask the Lord to fill you with His precious love from the very beginning.)

Lord, walk back through every second of my life during those early years. (If you were separated from parents because of sickness or death, some were born into families where they did not receive the love that was needed.) Lord Jesus, please go back and fill every void; give the love that was not received. Remove every hurt, every feeling of rejection. Take away all fears: fears of darkness, fears of falling, fears of animals, fears of being lost. I thank you Jesus for setting me free and for healing me.

I pray Lord that you will take my hand, go back in time, and walk to school with me. At times I felt so shy, so afraid to leave home and go into new situations. Jesus there were times I felt embarrassment or failure at school, will you take away those memories? When I was treated harshly by a teacher or I was hurt by classmates, please heal those hurts. Some fears entered during those first school years, fear of speaking in public, or fear of failure. Thank you for healing those hurts and for setting me free from those fears. I thank you and I praise you.

Lord Jesus, I thank you for my mother. (For those who did not have the love of a mother, please fill that void, that empty place and give them the love that was needed.) I ask you to stand between my mother and me and let your divine love flow between us. I ask forgiveness from my mother for any way I have hurt her or failed her, and I forgive her for any way she hurt or failed me.

Lord Jesus, I thank you for my dad. (For those who did not feel the love of an earthly dad, please give them all the love they needed but did not receive.) Stand between my dad and me. I pray that your divine love will mend any broken relationship. I ask forgiveness from my dad for any way I hurt or failed him, and I forgive him for any way he hurt or failed me.

I lift up my brothers and sisters to you. Where there were feelings of competition, jealousy, or resentment, I ask that your healing power and love mend every broken relationship. I forgive each brother and sister for hurting or failing me and I ask their forgiveness for the ways I hurt or failed them.

Thank you, Lord, for being there in my teenage years and when I was in Junior High and High School. There were new emotions and new fears. As each painful memory is brought to my mind, I pray that you will take a spiritual eraser and just wipe the pain from my mind and heal me. During those times that I tried things that were dangerous, I thank you for being there with your protective hand. Take away any feeling of humiliation, embarrassment, guilt, fear, or failure. (Some were teased because of race, appearance, size, or poverty and were wounded so deeply.) Let me know that you loved me and that you were there in every situation. (For those young people who experimented with drugs, which left their minds confused, Lord Jesus we pray you will repair the damage. Let them think clearly again; let them receive your healing. Let each one knows you love them and that you can redeem the past.)

As each of us started to leave home, there were new fears, frustrations, or hurts. (Some wanted to go on to college and were not able to; others were not able to enter the profession they dreamed of, and they felt such disappointment.) Jesus, heal every disappointment and every hurt.

Thank you for being there when we entered marriage. (For some it was such a beautiful new beginning.For others it was a nightmare.) Jesus, please take away every hurt. I pray that you will stand in between me and my mate and heal every hurt. I am saying to my mate, "I forgive you for hurting me and I ask your forgiveness for hurting you." Lord Jesus, through Your divine love, I thank you for mending every broken relationship, and wiping away every painful memory. (Where there has been the heartbreak of divorce and there are feelings of guilt, rejection, bitterness, and loneliness, take away all those negative feelings. Heal the deep wounds and erase the painful memories. Jesus, fill each mate with forgiveness, Your divine love and healing power.)

Thank you, Lord, for my children. Take away any feeling I have of failure or guilt as a parent. When I punished unwisely or was too possessive with my love, when words were spoken in criticism or anger, I pray you will heal any hurt that was caused. I ask their forgiveness and I forgive them for hurting me.

Lord, I thank you for being there during those terrifying times of accidents, those times of sickness or surgery. I ask you now to take away the horror, the fear, and the memory of the pain. Set me free from the trauma I felt. Thank you for being there during times of sorrow. I thank you for taking my hand and walking through the valley with me; I thank you for lifting the burden; I thank you for taking away my sorrow, my grief, and my mourning. I thank you for giving me your joy and your peace.

Now, Lord Jesus, thank you for walking back through every second of my life up to this exact moment. Thank you for healing me of all my hurts, my fears, my painful memories, and my guilt; for setting me free. Thank you for filling me with your love. Help me to love myself. Help me to love others. But most of all, Jesus, help me to love you as I should. I thank you for giving me joy. I thank you for giving me peace. Thank you, Jesus! I thank you for going down deep into the darkest recesses of my mind and cleansing me. I thank you for healing my mind, my emotions, and my memories. I thank you, Jesus, for making me whole; and I give you all the praise and all the glory. AMEN

<u>Letter to the Reader</u>

Dear Overcomer,

Thank you for reading and completing this book. It is my prayer that you have started on your healing journey, experienced healing in your life, and have found a new freedom in Jesus. It may have felt like a long journey to get to where you are, but I assure you, it is one that was worth it. After receiving inner healing- you will be like the lame who was healed enough to walk; and if at any time you experience some struggle, do not take that to mean the inner healing did not work. Continue to confess with your mouth the truth of your new life; and reject the old habit of automatically doubting every time you struggle. Also, do not assume that inner healing will lead to a painless life. Sometimes pain is not caused by bitter roots, it is just God testing and refining you. Remember you are not alone on this journey. God is with you, offering His love, grace, and strength every step of the way.

With heartfelt gratitude,

Myra Carden

Citations

[1]Weinstein, Lynn. "Business Reference Specialist, Science, Technology & Business: Black Wall Street in Tulsa, OK Destroyed on 6/1/1921." Library of Congress, Last Updated June 2022, https://guides.loc.gov/this-month-in-business-history/black-wall-street-destroyed#:~:text=On%20May%2031%20and%20June,communities%20in%20the%20United%20States.

[2]Williams Ph.D, Monnica T. "Colorblind Ideology Is a Form of Racism." Psychology Today, 2011, https://www.psychologytoday.com/us/blog/culturally-speaking/201112/colorblind-ideology-is-form-racism

[3] McDaniel, Eric; Moore, Elena (March 29, 2022). "Lynching is now a federal hate crime after a century of blocked efforts". NPR. Retrieved March 29, 2022.

Bitcon, Scott; http://www.greatbiblestudy.com/inner_healing_101.php Copyright © 2003-2008

Cook, Alison, MA, Ph.D. https://www.alisoncookphd.com/church-hurt-4-steps-healing/ BLOG

Conquer Series, https://conquerseries.com/science-confirms-bible-on-generational-curses/

Cornacchia, Deb *https*://www.christianhealingmin.org/

Dearing, Norma: *The Healing Touch* (Chosen Books, 2002). ISBN 0-8007-9302-1.

Dias, B. G., & Ressler, K. J. (2013). Parental olfactory experience influences behavior and neural structure in subsequent generations. *Nature Neuroscience, advanced online publication.* DOI:10.1038/nn.3594

Eivaz, Jennifer Inner Healing and Deliverance Handbook (Chosen Books 2022) ISBN 9780800799229

Frangipane, Francis, *The three battlegrounds.* Cedar Rapids, IA: Advancing Church Publications, 1989.

Gibson, Noel & Phyl, *Excuse Me, Your Rejection Is Showing* (Sovereign

World Publishers, Tonbridge, Kent TN 11 0ZS, England, 1997, reprinted 2004). ISBN 1-85240-110-9

Hogue, Rodney, *Liberated* (Destiny Publishers, 2019); & *Forgiveness (1997)* ISBN 978-164007440-8

Hayward, Chris, The *End of Rejection* (Regal Books, 2007), ISBN 0-8307-4317-0

Horrobin, Peter The Foundation and Practice of Deliverance Ministry *Healing Through Deliverance*(Sovereign World, 2008)

Inner Healing 10*1: Healing Emotional Wounds Jay Bartlett Copyright ©️ 2003-2008 Robert L.*

Kraft, Charles *Deep Wounds, Deep Healing* (Servant Pub., 1993). ISBN 0-89283-784-5.Counselling Australia, 2004.

Meyer, Joyce,   Beauty for Ashes

https://www.mayoclinic.org/diseases-conditions/anxiety/symptoms-causes/syc-20350961

Prince, Derek, *God's Remedy for Rejection* (Whitaker House, 1993). ISBN 088368-864-6

Rohrbaugh, Jamie, https://www.fromhispresence.com/4-signs-you-have-a-stronghold-of-rejection-and-abandonment

Sandford, John & Paula, *Healing the Wounded Spiri*t (Victory House, 1985). ISBN 0-932081-14-2.

Seamands, David, 1981, *Healing for Damaged Emotions*, Cook Publishing

Self, Nan Brown www.ForgivenessByGrace.com

Smith, Ed. PTSD https://www.transformationprayer.org/

Sudduth, William*, So Free,* (RAM Ministries, 1991) ISBN 0-9712520-1-7

https://www.timothytomlinson.org/single-post/2019/02/06/inner-heal-ing-and-deliverances-heals-fear-and-anxiety

Verny, Dr. Thomas The Secret Life of the Unborn Child (Dell Publishing 1981) ISBN 978-0-440-50565-5

White, John, *Eros Redeemed: breaking the stranglehold of sexual sin.* Downers Grove, Ill: InterVarsity Press, 1993.

Wiles, Jeremy. "Soul Refiner" Blog. Published June 22, 2022. https://blog.soulrefiner.com/science-confirms-bible-on-generational-curses

Yehuda, R *et al* (2005). Transgenerational Effects of Posttraumatic Stress Disorder in Babies of Mothers Exposed to the World Trade Center Attacks during Pregnancy. *Journal of Clinical Endocrinology & Metabolism*, DOI: 10.1210/jc.2005-0550

Article: http://www.prayercounselling.com/counselling/lesson6.php

www.ingramcontent.com/pod-product-compliance
Lightning Source LLC
Chambersburg PA
CBHW060914120626
46553CB00001B/326